prayer
weapons

prayer weapons

ALLEGRA HARRAH

Fleming H. Revell Company
Old Tappan, New Jersey

Library of Congress Cataloging in Publication Data

Harrah, Allegra.
    Prayer weapons.

    1. Prayer. 2. Christian life—Baptist authors.
I. Title.
BV210.2.H365   248'.48'61   75-29426
ISBN 0-8007-0773-7

This book is dedicated to my husband, Cal. Words are not adequate to express my appreciation to him for his love and care these many years. This study has been hammered into existence by the two of us in the midst of living the daily joys and struggles of a minister and wife rearing eight children in the parsonage. The lessons of this book are deeply etched on both of our minds. He has taught me, counseled me, sustained me with his prayers, and left me free to write. I will always be grateful.

Contents

Foreword

In November of 1969, the Reverend and Mrs. Cal Harrah came to the staff of the First Baptist Church in Van Nuys, California, where for sixteen years it was my privilege to be the pastor. From the very first day they set foot on our campus, they have had a spiritual ministry among our people that has resulted in souls being saved, lives being changed, and Christians experiencing phenomenal growth both in grace and in the knowledge of our Lord and Saviour, Jesus Christ.

Mrs. Harrah, affectionately called Allegra by all who know her, has for the past three years been teaching a Wednesday-morning Ladies' Bible Class. It has grown so much that they finally had to move out of our largest assembly hall—accommodating five hundred—into our main sanctuary. Each Wednesday morning, women from practically every church in the San Fernando Valley flock to hear the teaching of God's Word by this lovely, dedicated, and gifted lady. Hundreds of these today testify to manifold spiritual blessings which have come into their lives as the result of Allegra's sharing the Word with them. Only eternity will reveal the good that she has accomplished through this class.

In the course of their years of serving Christ in Van Nuys, they have led many seminars dealing with the prayer weapons which God has made available to His children with which to fight the adversary. As people have applied this teaching in combating the enemy, they have found the secret of living the

Christian life victoriously. To use the language of today's teen-agers, "They have really been turned on for Christ as a result of this." Consequently they have been and are most productive in their witnessing for the Saviour.

This book *Prayer Weapons* is the result of long hours of prayerful research which Allegra and Cal invested in their preparation for their seminars. Not only is it based upon sound biblical exegesis, but also upon the actual experience of putting the weapons to the test as they themselves have used them in fighting Satan.

I am thankful that the Holy Spirit led Allegra to bring this volume into being. I look forward to having a copy of it in my library as a reference book to which I shall often refer. I recom-mend to you as a Christian that you add it to your book collec-tion. You will find it an invaluable asset in guiding you in your struggle against that one whose supreme desire is to destroy you.

HAROLD L. FICKETT, JR.

Preface

"This doesn't sound like the States. It sounds like China where Satan has so much power."

My husband and I were in a situation where we had seen God bless so marvelously. We had seen many come to Christ, and were experiencing the joys of body-life as a group. In the midst of this, things began to happen. We saw a group which had known much blessing begin to turn on each other, and much heartache followed.

During this time a missionary just returning from China visited in our home. We were sharing with her God's blessings on the group, and also the present difficulties. It was then that she made the comment about Satan and his power. We began searching the Scriptures and were reminded that in some areas Christ could do nothing "because of their unbelief" (*see* Matthew 13:58 KJV). Some cities had become hardened to the Gospel, and very little work could be done in them. It is true today as it was then.

Her statement was used to start us on a study of prayer. We had been praying together every day—and still things fell apart. We believed there was a Satan, but were not aware of his position or power. We realized that there must be a great deal more to prayer than we knew.

After twenty years of study on this subject, I still feel we have only scratched the surface. If we only knew and appropriated the power available to us, what a difference this would make in our lives.

I believe that in order to really communicate with someone, you must know him. One can pass the time of day, discuss the weather or the headlines in the daily paper, but it requires a deeper level of friendship to share one's inner feelings.

For this reason, the book begins with three chapters on the Trinity—God the Father, God the Son, and God the Holy Spirit. It is not, of course, a complete study, as one cannot comprehend the deep truths of the Trinity in three chapters.

However, as we begin to learn about the Trinity as a preface to prayer, we will through prayer learn more about the Trinity. As we learn more about the Father we pray to, we will open up more to Him. As we are more honest with Him in prayer, we will see more of our prayers answered. As we know Him more, we trust Him more. The love between us broadens and deepens —*His* love, of course. As His love fills us and enlarges our vision, we become more bold in prayer. We ask, knowing we will receive, because He said so.

We trust that as you read, the Holy Spirit will teach and will answer your prayers, ". . . exceeding abundantly above all that we ask or think, according to the power that worketh in us" (Ephesians 3:20 KJV).

I am greatly indebted to the authors of many books who have contributed much to my life. I am also indebted to the many who have supported us spiritually and prayed this book into being.

I would especially like to thank Gwen Waggoner who spent many hours typing the manuscript copy.

ALLEGRA HARRAH

prayer weapons

1

God the Father

"I really try to pray, but I'm not getting anywhere."

"I did pray, but things got worse, so I quit."

"There are too many things to pray about, and I get so discouraged I quit."

These are typical remarks which we hear as we discuss prayer. I understand all three remarks because I've experienced those feelings. I've been discouraged—have felt as if I were getting nowhere and have felt there were just too many things about which to pray!

God—our Father—is interested in people in these circumstances. He always meets us in our need. Do you remember that Thomas was not willing to believe that Christ really rose from the grave unless he saw with his own eyes the nail prints in Christ's hands? In fact, he insisted that he would have to put his finger into the print of the nails and thrust his hand into His side before he would believe.

Of course, Jesus knew what Thomas said, and met him at his point of doubt. When He came again into the room with the disciples, He greeted them: "Peace be with you," and turned immediately to Thomas, saying, "Reach here your finger, and see My hands; and reach here your hand, and put it into My side; and be not unbelieving, but believing" (John 20:27). Thomas answered, and it must have been with awe, "My Lord and my God!" (v. 28). I believe Thomas's faith was strengthened that day as he looked at Jesus, for he trusted God and people in a new way from that day on.

God the Father, the First Person of the Trinity, is a loving God. He is also a just God and allows us to reap the results of our sin and rejection of Him. At the same time, He is a very merciful God who sent His Son, Jesus Christ, to seek and to save those who were lost (Luke 19:10). We also read: "The Lord is not slow about His promise, as some count slowness, but is patient toward you, not wishing for any to perish but for all to come to repentance" (2 Peter 3:9).

God's Love and Forgiveness   If from your childhood training you know only the judgment of God, your view of Him will be harsh. So many of us were taught the fear of God without a teaching of His love.

The first thing a child knows from a loving, human father is love. He will know it from the tone of voice and the feel of his arms. The relationship in the first year sets the stage for the relationships to come later between father and child. The importance of that first relationship cannot be overemphasized. If the father truly loves, there will be discipline, but only after a love relationship is established. A child who knows only harshness, cruel arms and hands, and a cross voice, has been exposed to the groundwork which produces a troubled child who will eventually become a troubled teenager and adult. It sets the pattern for the vicious cycle of rejection which repeats itself, generation after generation, until a heart reaches out to the God who is also reaching out, and the cycle is thereby broken. As we abide in Christ, God heals the pattern of rejection.

The Father-God of the Old Testament is the same God revealed in the New. In the Old Testament we see God's love for the Israelites whom He sought out while they continued to reject Him. I believe He watched with anguish each time they reaped the results of their sin and were taken into bondage. Again and again He called them back to Himself, always ready to forgive those who sought forgiveness.

In Luke 15 we have the beautiful picture of the father with the wayward son. The son had misused the father's trust, he had broken his father's heart with his waywardness, and had reaped the result of his rebellion and sin.

Nevertheless, when he did want to go back to the father, the son found the father watching for him with open arms. Also, his former position in the home was still as before. Their relationship was the same as it always was. The fellowship had been broken, but it was restored with a hug. He was cleaned up, given new clothing, and as if this weren't enough, the father prepared a banquet for the son who had returned. Nothing had taken the special place of the son in the father's heart.

God said to Moses: "Behold, there is a place by Me . . ." (Exodus 33:21). I believe there is a special place next to His heart that is ours and only ours. No one else can fit in our exact place.

This love is pictured throughout the Scriptures—a holy, righteous God—the Father who reaches down, lifts up to Himself, and redeems with His love. We read:

I waited patiently for the Lord;
And He inclined to me, and heard my cry.
He brought me up out of the pit of destruction, out of the
    miry clay;
And He set my feet upon a rock making my footsteps firm.
And He put a new song in my mouth, a song of praise to
    our God;
Many will see and fear,
And will trust in the Lord.

                                                   Psalms 40:1–3

Human Father Love   Let's talk about *human* father love. I don't know what these words mean to you. Perhaps they are empty phrases or they produce bitter memories? We approach

these words *father love* from our own frame of reference because the words have a different meaning for each of us.

Fathering a child does not give a father compassion any more
than education assures a man of wisdom. You may be one to
whom these words bring only memories of the opposite of love
—harshness, beatings, loneliness, emptiness—the knowledge
that the one you wanted to please so much was never pleased
with you. It may be that your father really did fail you.

Let's establish the fact now that each parent loves to the best
of his ability. I acknowledge as a parent of eight grown children
that I have made many mistakes, but I believe that at each time
I was performing to the best of my ability and according to the
light and insight I had at that particular time. I do, however,
reap the results of my mistakes. Nevertheless, God gives forgiveness and we build on our yesterdays. With the help of God's
love, those mistakes of the past become stepping-stones.

If you are one to whom the words *father love* bring sweet
memories of a father's arms, his lap, and his tender care, you are
very blessed. Prayer to our Heavenly Father will come much
more naturally to you.

In Ephesians we read: "Honor your father and mother (which
is the first commandment with a promise), that it may be well
with you, and that you may live long on the earth" (6:2, 3).
These are disturbing verses to most of us because if we are
honest we will acknowledge that our relationships with our
parents have been disappointing in some areas. In some in-
stances, the reactions are sharp and accusing.

I do believe God knows and understands our feelings as He
gives us this basic rule to honor our fathers and our mothers. In
fact, it was so important to God that He gave two rewards that
would follow as a result of obeying Him. The first: it will be well
with us. That is, we will prosper in every area—spiritually,
physically, and materially. The second promise states that we
will live long on the earth. Many are looking for the fountain of
youth and God promises it to us as we obey Him by honoring

our fathers and our mothers.

Now, I believe that none of us can honor our father and mother as God would have us do it. We have been hurt or rejected too much. I believe that the Holy Spirit will do this in and through us as we are open to His working in our lives. He is in us, ". . . both to will and to work for His good pleasure" (Philippians 2:13).

Let me give an illustration: Scripture says we are to honor those in authority over us (1 Timothy 2:2). We are to honor the office. I may not approve of all the President is doing (*see* Romans 13:1–7), but I honor and pray for the office. We likewise view the office, as it were, of mother and father. I may not approve of my parents or the way they reared me. In fact, they may have rejected me completely, but I honor the office. It does not say to love or understand. It says to *honor.*

We read in Hebrews: "See to it that no one comes short of the grace of God; that no root of bitterness springing up causes trouble, and by it many be defiled" (12:15). God knows that if we retain any bitterness toward our parents and what they have done to us, this bitterness will trouble us and defile many.

The Root of Bitterness   A root is spread out underground. It pushes upward—where it can be seen—and then branches out. This picture is used to describe bitterness. It cannot be hidden. As in Proverbs, "For as he thinks within himself, so is he" (23:7). Both the Bible and some modern psychologists teach that we are what we think, not what we say. The Scripture says we deceive ourselves. We think we are giving a completely different picture of ourselves than we are actually giving. What is being seen is the real us—what we really think, and our true attitudes toward life are openly revealed.

There is a test for knowing your true personality. That is— what you think about most. You should search your heart to see what most occupies your mind. This is the real you and will reveal your goals and priorities.

I used to believe that I could close the door on my yesterdays
—just bury them and start with today—but I don't believe that
now. I believe as in Ephesians 6:2, 3 that if there is any bitterness in my parental relationships, whether my parents are living or dead, it will affect all my present relationships. Hebrews
12:15 reminds me that it will trouble me and defile many. My
bitterness, as a root, is reaching up and out—touching every life
I touch.

Have you ever shared a bitter area, hoping for some help,
only to be told, "Go have your devotions," or "Just have faith"?
Sometimes we feel that we should be mature enough as Christians to bury our feelings or to "live above them" or "get on the
victory side." This is only burying the problem.

I believe that bitterness and other emotions need to be ver-
balized, not ignored or buried. Some teach that if we realize we
hate our mother we should go and tell her. I do not. I believe
we should be honest with God and verbalize our feelings to
Him. God knows our feelings, although we may wish that He
did not!

Please take two pieces of paper and write down the name
FATHER on one and MOTHER on the other. Then list all the
emotions you feel toward them. No one is going to see the list
except God and you, so be honest about your attitudes. Perhaps
you will want to start with love, or perhaps you will wish to
begin with hatred. Remember that there are many faces to love
and hate. Search your heart, and let the Holy Spirit do His work.
You may find resentments and hostilities buried there. If so,
write them down. This is scriptural therapy. In order to write
them, you have to let them surface from the subconscious
(where we have buried them) to the conscious. This is actually
bringing our problems into focus. Once they are in focus and
have been named, we can deal with them.

When your lists are complete, as far as you know, place them
on your Bible. This is in reality: "Casting all your anxiety upon
Him, because He cares for you" (1 Peter 5:7). Talk to God in

prayer, confessing the things you have written down. The gift
of forgiveness for others and ourselves comes only from Him.
Sometimes we feel that we have such a right to bitterness in the
flesh that we will not let go of it even though we recognize it.
I believe then, as we tell God we are willing to let Him take it,
He pulls the plug and drains the bitterness away. He cannot do
this work unless you allow Him. He will not go against your will.
You may keep your bitterness if you wish, but by keeping it you
will have the results—it will trouble you and defile many.

Look around you. Bitterness cannot be hidden. We see it in
the lines on a person's face, we hear it in the tone of voice, and
see it in the eyes and the smile. People with bitterness become
more bitter as the years go by because it grows (a root) and fills
the one involved.

After you have prayed over your papers, then burn or destroy
them, as this should be only between you and God. Later, as you
start to work on this problem, again you will remember that you
wrote it down, placed it on your Bible and burned or destroyed
it. You have truly given it to God to work out.

You can then praise God for answered prayer:

Be anxious for nothing, but in everything by prayer and
supplication with thanksgiving let your requests be made
known to God. And the peace of God, which surpasses all
comprehension, shall guard your hearts and your minds
in Christ Jesus.

Philippians 4:6, 7

God gives another promise: "When my father and my mother
forsake me, then the Lord will take me up" (Psalms 27:10 KJV).

I do believe this is literally true. When we can face and name
our emotions, we can, in Christ, deal with them. When we can
face the fact that our parents did in reality forsake us or neglect
us or whatever, we can ask God to take us up in His arms and

fill that which we lacked in normal father-mother love. We read: "The eternal God is a dwelling place, And underneath are the everlasting arms . . ." (Deuteronomy 33:27).

We remind ourselves that our parents have loved us to the best of their ability, and if we are hung up on their attitudes toward us, that is our problem, not theirs. Parents must give an account for all they have done to their children, but we as children must give an account for our attitudes toward our parents. God brings us back to one of His basic rules—Honor thy father and thy mother and it will be well with you. All other problems will work out as you follow His procedures. Long life is an added blessing. Bitterness, resentments, and hostilities *do* affect our health. They grow as a cancer affecting more and more of the body. And they do control our attitudes toward other people.

Acceptance Begins With God   You will understand much more about your situation if you will recall the types of homes in which your mother and father were reared. We are patterned and programmed by the things that have happened to us. Since we *are* what we think, we will put those same patterns on others unless we let God move across our lives to change them.

God's harvesting rule comes into play here: "Be not deceived; God is not mocked; for whatsoever a man soweth, that shall he reap" (Galatians 6:7 KJV). If we give out negative thoughts, we receive negative thoughts. If we were never accepted as children, we have no pattern for acceptance. Thus, we cannot accept ourselves or our children. The pattern moves from generation to generation and from person to person unless we allow God to move across and change the pattern.

Acceptance starts with God, as does love. "We love, because He first loved us" (1 John 4:19). Love starts with God and comes down through us and goes back to God.

In Ephesians: ". . . he hath made us accepted in the beloved"

(1:6 KJV). I love this verse, for no matter what my situation or problem I am accepted by Him. We approach Him with our feelings of fear and failure and He reminds us that we are accepted in Him. Many times we will argue the point, reminding Him of our wrongdoings. In fact, many of us become martyrs to our own little crosses of guilt and try to pay our own price for our sins. We need to be delivered from our religious fetishes and brought into the largeness of His forgiveness and acceptance.

We cannot accept anyone else until we accept ourselves. This is perhaps the most difficult problem of all. Acceptance begins with God. As we read and reread Ephesians 1:6, the Holy Spirit patterns these words into our minds, and the reprogramming of the Word begins. This is what God means when He says, "This book of the law shall not depart from your mouth, but you shall meditate on it day and night, so that you may be careful to do according to all that is written in it; for then you will make your way prosperous, and then you will have [good] success" (Joshua 1:8). Our minds are actually reprogrammed by the Holy Spirit through the Word, and our lives are changed. We do prosper and have good success because of our reprogramming by the Word.

As we begin to believe that we are accepted, we begin to accept ourselves—and then we can accept others. We do not have a need to judge them or try to change or mold them. We accept them because of the Holy Spirit's work in us.

God not only has arms around us (Deuteronomy 33:27), but He also holds our hand:

> The steps of a man are established by the Lord;
> And He delights in his way.
> When he falls, he shall not be hurled headlong;
> Because the Lord is the One who holds his hand.
>
> Psalms 37:23, 24

This man is a believer in Christ. You will find it interesting to take a concordance and look up the verses on *arm* and *hand*. They are used often in connection with our relationship with God and give added strength and stability to our lives. This is important if we have not remembered a father's arm and hand from childhood. We need this programmed into our minds.

God also tells us that nothing can separate us from His love and this is *so* important in our Father relationship. Many of us have been separated from *human* father love and need to know this perfect love of God. In Romans 8:38, 39 we read: "For I am convinced that neither death, nor life, nor angels, nor principalities, nor things present, nor things to come, nor powers, nor height, nor depth, nor any other created thing, shall be able to separate us from the love of God, which is in Christ Jesus our Lord." I love the way the Living Bible quotes this passage. "For I am convinced that nothing can ever separate us from his love. Death can't, and life can't. The angels won't, and all the powers of hell itself cannot keep God's love away. Our fears for today, our worries about tomorrow, or where we are—high above the sky, or in the deepest ocean—nothing will ever be able to separate us from the love of God demonstrated by our Lord Jesus Christ when he died for us."

Romans 5:5 has become a very important verse in my life. After about twenty-five years of ministry here in the States, our family went to Germany with our four younger children. One of our older daughters was married and the other three were in college. Cal, my husband, was to take the ministry of Youth for Christ to teenagers of military families stationed in Europe. We felt that because we were older we would have fewer adjustments than younger overseas workers. We were wrong!

After the initial excitement wore off, the family began to get depressed. Cal no longer had the identity and involvement of the ministry. I was no longer a minister's wife. The phone was not ringing and the calendar was not filled with engagements. The children had left their friends and familiar schools, as well as four brothers and sisters.

Now, I know that some teach that Christians should not be depressed, for depression is sin. Whatever it may be, a loss of identity or cultural shock, it can really play tricks on the mind and personality.

In the middle of all this, I grew cold inside. I was sure that no one really cared for me. I know now that they all loved me to the best of their ability. They, too, were adjusting. However, I was continually aware of the reality of my depression.

I found myself not only capable of hating, but *really* hating. I couldn't believe it when God really showed me my true condition. I had always thought that I had at least some love for people, and now I really saw how much of that was superficial. God dipped me far enough into depression and coldness so that I would understand others, and then He delivered me from it. He gave me this verse: ". . . the love of God has been poured out within our hearts through the Holy Spirit who was given to us" (Romans 5:5). Even when there is no love—only coldness—the Holy Spirit pours God's love through us and we are warmed and His love reaches out to others through us. It was beautiful. God did this for me and through me. He also began opening doors for us and did many marvelous things.

The Abiding Presence   God gives a special place of abiding and hiding in Him. In Psalms 91:4 we read: ". . . under His wings you may seek refuge. . . ." This draws a beautiful picture of the mother hen, lifting her wings so that the little chicks can cuddle under them, close to her. She is the one who takes the wind and rain and acts as a family shelter, not they.

Each of us needs a nest to which we can return—a place that is familiar and dear, that gives security. Many of us do not have that earthly nest. Dear ones have gone on. God Himself says, "Under His wings you may seek refuge," and as we draw near to Him as our Heavenly Father and hide under His wings, we are sheltered and we are comforted.

We read in Hebrews: "Let your way of life be free from the love of money, being content with what you have; for He Himself has said, 'I will never desert you, nor will I ever forsake you' " (13:5). Many of us have been left as children. We live with an unspoken and often unacknowledged fear that we will be left again. As you read and reread this verse, God will program into your mind the security of His love and presence.

His presence comes in to abide when we accept Christ Jesus as Saviour. He walks with us always. From Psalm 23 we know that He walks with us as we leave this earth to go to be with Him. He is Light, and because He is with us our passing is not in darkness. The Scripture refers to shadows, but in order to have shadows there must be light. The Father's arms are around us. His hand is holding ours—a beautiful feeling of security.

This loving Father is the One to whom we pray. Please read these verses on His *Father love* several times a day and you will begin to realize that you are very precious to God and that He loves you. Perhaps you are not aware that even outside of Christ Jesus you have worth. We are told this in Ephesians:

> But God, being rich in mercy, because of His great love with which He loved us, even when we were dead in our transgressions, made us alive together with Christ (by grace you have been saved), and raised us up with Him, and seated us with Him in the heavenly places, in Christ Jesus.
>
> Ephesians 2:4–6

Even when we were dead in sins, He loved us. We were not worthless. We were unworthy of salvation, but not worthless. In Christ we are worthy. We need that balance or we will feel always unworthy and a failure.

In Psalm 23 we read: "The Lord is my shepherd." We all need to lean upon someone—someone who is ours. Some of us don't have anyone here to give us this security, but with Him we have that security. The Lord is my Shepherd. He is mine!

2

Jesus Christ—Our Saviour
and Bridegroom

God the Father, the One we have just been talking about, is a part of the Trinity. He refers to Himself as being Three. Three Beings and yet One—God the Father, God the Son, and God the Holy Spirit.

God the Father created the heavens and the earth. We know from John 1 that Jesus was there with Him at that time. God created the heavens and the earth and said, "It is good." The earth was created without sin. War, sickness, and death were not a part of God's plan for this planet.

Even though the earth was created without sin, Satan, in his present form, was there in the Garden. Satan used the deceiving, questioning methods he still uses today. He beguiled Eve and she in turn tempted her husband, and they disobeyed God. The Fall was not a part of God's plan. God must have longed that they not listen to Satan. God had given them a free will. He had given them the ability to accept Him or reject Him. They chose to reject, and with the decision came the results— separation from God (Genesis 3).

All mankind was God's possession. He had made us. However, now the race was separated from Him as a result of sin. With His unfailing love He continued to love—and longed to have fellowship again.

In the Old Testament He provided a way for fellowship through sacrifice. In the New Testament we see God, having made His plans from the beginning, bringing them to pass. He made His plans from the beginning, bringing them to pass. He sent His Son, Jesus Christ, to take the punishment for our sins. A price had to be paid. The belonging was lost and had to be bought back again. This is the meaning of redemption. Jesus, His Son, my Saviour, left all the riches of heaven, took on a body, and became man that He might be my Redeemer.

> Have this attitude in yourselves which was also in Christ Jesus, who, although He existed in the form of God, did not regard equality with God a thing to be grasped, but emptied Himself, taking the form of a bond-servant, and being made in the likeness of men.
>
> Philippians 2:5–7

The Supreme Price of Redemption   To redeem means to buy back something that was yours, to free someone from danger. Jesus Christ paid the ransom. This means the price for my freedom. As I become one with Him, I am freed from Satan's bondage—his lies, his deceivings, and death as his slave. I am freed to new life, eternal life in heaven, and all of His riches. I am freed from my past, its failures and its chains that bind.

Jesus Christ, being my substitute, paid the supreme price —His life in place of mine. I do not understand the mystery of the cross and Jesus as my substitute. I do not understand how His death on the cross made my salvation possible. Neither do I understand that there is really only one way to be born on this planet and one way to leave it. Argue it as we may, there is still only one way to enter this earth and one way to depart. There are so many things that are mysterious about life and death. There are so many things about the planets and space that we do not understand. We accept them as facts. God created it all. He authorized the Bible that we might know the truth of God.

But just as it is written,
  "Things which eye has not seen and ear has not heard,
  And which have not entered the heart of man,
  All that God has prepared for those who love Him."
For to us God revealed them through the Spirit; for the
Spirit searches all things, even the depths of God.

                                                    1 Corinthians 2:9, 10

This we do know as we read and believe the Word—Jesus, my
Saviour, took upon Himself the form of man, that He—as man
—might pay the price, once and for all, for the sin of Adam and
Eve and their descendants (Romans 5:12-21). Therefore we do
not need to keep on paying the price for this inherited spiritual
blood disease.

"Truly, truly, I say to you, he who hears My word, and believes Him who sent Me, has eternal life, and does not come into
judgment, but has passed out of death into life" (John 5:24).

Has is present tense—a possession. The knowledge that "As
far as the east is from the west, so far hath he removed our
transgressions from us," comforts us (Psalms 103:12 KJV). God,
in the form of His Son, took our guilt. Remember that He took
it. He desires that we not use our unresolved guilt as nails to
crucify ourselves on our own little crosses. God the Father
created the world and man. God sent Jesus to save us from sin
and the resulting sins of this planet.

Christ the Bridegroom   God also tells us in the Word that He
is sending this same Jesus, our dearly beloved Bridegroom, back
for us. In Luke 5:34, 35, Luke 12:35-40, and Mark 2:19, 20 Jesus
is referred to as the Bridegroom. In John 3:28-30 John the
Baptist also refers to Christ as the Bridegroom. He reminds us
that there is joy in the presence of Christ the Bridegroom. To
hear His voice brings joy.

Shortly after Jesus' terrible death on the cross, He was laid in
a tomb. Later, as the two Marys went to the grave, they found

an angel who told them that Jesus was not there. He had risen! The body was gone! After His Resurrection, He appeared to His disciples. He walked the road to Emmaus with two men and was seen by others. He gave them His final instructions. They were to wait in Jerusalem until power from God filled them. He had promised that the Holy Spirit would come (John 15:26).

In Luke 24 we are told that after Jesus spoke His last words He blessed them, and as He was blessing them His body began to go up. He ascended until a cloud covered Him. His work was done. They were filled with a great holy joy. I think it is beautiful that in this moment, as their beloved One left, God sent two angelic beings to His followers. They were not alone. They were told that Jesus had gone to heaven, and would someday come back in just the same way He had left.

He, my beloved Jesus, is indeed the Saviour of the world. Jesus was killed, rose again, and ascended into heaven—and will return in the same way. He is our beloved Bridegroom.

Christ uses a beautiful object lesson to illustrate a spiritual truth in John 15. The setting is a vineyard. He sets the stage for His story by naming those who participate. He says that He is the Vine and His Father is the Caretaker of the vineyard (v. 1). He tells us that we, the believers, His bride, are the branches on the Vine (v. 5).

This is a passage on relationships and their results. The Bridegroom—Christ—and His bride—the church—are beautifully pictured here. He says, "You did not choose Me, but I chose you, and appointed you, that you should go and bear fruit, and that your fruit should remain, that whatever you ask of the Father in My name, He may give to you" (v. 16).

Let's think of one appointed for an official position by our government, such as an ambassador. He is chosen for his position and delegated to go with a particular message to a certain place. He has a vital position in representing our government and is given a certain task to perform. The success of his responsibility does not depend on whether or not he is popular with people, but upon his faithfulness in doing the job for which he was chosen.

Christ the Bridegroom chose us, the bride, and we have the resulting responsibility to bear fruit. In fact, He wants it to be strong, healthy fruit—fruit that will last.

Cleansed by the Word   The bride in this story is clean: "You are already clean because of the word which I have spoken to you" (John 15:3). She has been cleansed by the Word. We have learned from Ephesians 5:26—". . . He might sanctify her [the church], having cleansed her by the washing of water with the word"—that Christ wants His bride not to have spots or wrinkles. She is to be holy and pure. He says, "Sanctify them through thy truth: thy word is truth" (John 17:17 KJV). Christ becomes our holiness. He cleansed us with His Blood. "But if we walk in the light as He Himself is in the light, we have fellowship with one another, and the blood of Jesus His Son cleanses us from all sin" (1 John 1:7).

This branch, the bride, has been chosen and cleansed by Him for the purpose of bearing fruit. There are some requirements necessary to accomplish this. We are told that the first one is that the bride, the church, must abide (or live) in the Vine.

"Abide in Me"   In John 15:4 Jesus says, "Abide in Me, and I in you. . . ." Remember that 1 Corinthians 6:17 teaches us that we are one spirit with Him. This is the beautiful spirit union of John 15: *Abide in Me, and I in you*—one spirit.

In the physical relationship of marriage pictured in Ephesians 5:22–33, the two people become one body (v. 31). In the spiritual relationship of the Vine and the branch, of the Bridegroom and the bride, we become one spirit. In either case, there are the results of oneness—the oneness of two bodies coming together, and the oneness of two spirits, Christ's and ours. Actually, the spirit within us which becomes one spirit name cast out demons, and in Your name perform many miracles?" And then I will declare to them, "I never knew you; Depart from Me, you who practice lawlessness."

Matthew 7:20–23

These pictured here were not Christ's own at all. There had been no union. They had simply taken on a role of godliness and were performing services in the energy of the flesh. The deception was conceived in the mind, and the body brought the works to pass. The works did not stand.

This truth of abiding or living in Him is so important that He continues. He tells us that this togetherness brings much fruit (spiritual), reminding us again that apart from Him we can do nothing (John 15:5). Our lives are sterile!

Jesus therefore answered and was saying to them, "Truly, truly, I say to you, the Son can do nothing of Himself, unless it is something He sees the Father doing; for whatever the Father does, these things the Son also does in like manner."

John 5:19

Philip said to Him, "Lord, show us the Father, and it is enough for us." Jesus said to him, "Have I been so long with you, and yet you have not come to know Me, Philip? He who has seen Me has seen the Father; how do you say, 'Show us the Father'? Do you not believe that I am in the Father, and the Father is in Me? The words that I say to you I do not speak on My own initiative, but the Father abiding in Me does His works. Believe Me that I am in the Father, and the Father in Me; otherwise believe on account of the works themselves. Truly, truly, I say to you, he who believes in Me, the works that I do shall he with His, as we abide in Him, is the Spirit of God Himself. "Je. answered and said to him, 'If anyone loves Me, he will keep N word; and My Father will love him, and We will come to hin and make Our abode with him' " (John 14:23).

The holy, pure Spirit of Christ does not become one spirit with any of our old human nature. It is His Holy Spirit in us answering the wooing, loving Spirit of the Father that fellowships together in oneness. He tells us in John 15:4 that the branch cannot bear life (fruit) unless it is a part of the Vine. In the human relationship, a person can long for human fruit of the body (a child), but it is impossible alone. The laws of nature dictate that there must be a union. This is also true spiritually. Christ says, "Neither can you unless you abide in Me." As far as any fruit that we may bear in our service for Him—trying to do it by ourselves and in our own way is as nothing. It will not be fruit that will remain.

I knew a lady many years ago who desperately wanted a child. She and her husband planned and dreamed, but all to no avail. After several years of this, she one day announced that she was going to have a child. They were delighted. During the months that followed, her body changed and took on the appearance of a pregnant woman. However, as the doctor watched, he was anxious. He finally had to tell her that it was a false pregnancy, and that the baby had been conceived only in her mind. She had wanted a child so much that her mind had brought to pass the changes in her body. This was devastating. She had to have special treatment and care.

Do you suppose this is like the case of those showing the fruit of their works to Christ in the last day?

So then, you will know them by their fruits. Not every one who says to Me, "Lord, Lord," will enter the kingdom of heaven; but he who does the will of My Father who is in heaven. Many will say to Me on that day, "Lord, Lord, did we not prophesy in Your name, and in Your do also; and greater works than these shall he do; because I go to the Father."

John 14:8–12

"If anyone does not abide in Me, he is thrown away as a branch, and dries up; and they gather them, and cast them into the fire, and they are burned."

John 15:6

He is speaking here of a person. The King James Version says, "If a man abide not in me, he is cast forth as a branch, and is withered; and men gather them, and cast them into the fire, and they are burned." Jesus is not referring to a branch, but to a man—a person hiding in the branches trying to look like one.

Cal and I pruned a vine the other day. As we cleaned out the dead branches we noticed that so much of their growth was hidden behind the green vines. Some of the dead branches had put their "feelers" around the green branches so securely that they seemed to be one branch. Jesus tells us that anyone playing the role and not really abiding in the Vine will be separated for eternity from Him. There is no union.

"If you abide in Me, and My words abide in you, ask whatever you wish, and it shall be done for you" (John 15:7). He tells us that one of the results of abiding, of being one spirit with Him, will be answered prayer. *Ask whatever you wish, and it shall be done for you.* A person may delight in his relationship with Christ, and we read: "Delight yourself in the Lord; And He will give you the desires of your heart" (Psalms 37:4).

He also tells us that our bearing much fruit as a result of abiding brings God glory. "My true disciples produce bountiful harvests. This brings great glory to my Father" (John 15:8 LB). Matthew 5:16 reads: "Let your light shine before men in such a way that they may see your good works, and glorify your Father who is in heaven."

Christ said, "I glorified Thee on the earth, having accomplished the work which Thou hast given Me to do" (John 17:4). He set the example for us. He is always our example, but remember that He is much more than that. He is Jesus Christ, the Son of God, our Saviour.

Love and Obedience   We read further: "Just as the Father has loved Me, I have also loved you; abide in My love" (John 15:9). He reveals a startling truth—He loves us with the same love God has for Him and asks us to abide (nest) in that. I cannot fathom the depths of this love. This is the love that reaches down and draws us through Calvary to Himself.

He asks for our obedience: "If you keep My commandments [and then the result] you will abide in My love. [He set the example.] I have kept My Father's commandments, and abide in His love" (John 15:10).

> "But that the world may know that I love the Father, and as the Father gave Me commandment, even so I do. . . ."
>
> John 14:31

> "But I will freely do what the Father requires of me so that the world will know that I love the Father. . . ."
>
> John 14:31 LB

There are other verses to describe His love: "If you love Me, you will keep My commandments" (John 14:15). "He who has My commandments and keeps them, he it is who loves Me; and he who loves Me shall be loved by My Father, and I will love him, and will disclose Myself to him" (John 14:21). "Greater love has no one than this, that one lay down his life for his friends" (John 15:13).

He describes love—*Greater love has no one than this, that*

one lay down his life for his friends. One cannot imagine any greater love nor any love more sacrificial.

Then He defines who His friends are (John 15:14, 15). They are those who do His will, and He establishes their position. They are not slaves—they are friends. A slave does not know what his master is doing but these people knew what Jesus was doing. Jesus had taken His disciples into an inner circle of relationship. They were chosen and ordained to be God's own beloved, His bride.

Love One Another   "A new commandment I give to you, that you love one another, even as I have loved you, that you also love one another. By this all men will know that you are My disciples, if you have love for one another" (John 13:34, 35).

In John 15:11 He gives us another of the results of abiding in His love. He gives us His joy and He wants it to be overflowing joy. Don't you love to see a joyful Christian! This is not something obtained by itself; it is a result of abiding.

Jesus goes back to love. In verse 10 He has said, "If you keep My commandments, you will abide in My love." In verse 12 He gives us this commandment: "This is My commandment, that you love one another, just as I have loved you." In verse 17 He commands us one more time to love one another. I believe this thrills the heart of God as He sees His love flowing through us —one to another. ". . . the love of God has been poured out within our hearts through the Holy Spirit who was given to us" (Romans 5:5).

The fruit born in our lives—as we are the branches—will be the work of the Holy Spirit within us. When we are alive in Christ—there will be fruit. "Therefore if any man is in Christ, he is a new creature; the old things passed away; behold, new things have come" (2 Corinthians 5:17).

In Galatians 5:22, 23 we read: "But the fruit of the Spirit is love, joy, peace, patience, kindness, goodness, faithfulness, gentleness, self-control. . . ." No more can you and I bear these good works by ourselves than that dear lady could have a baby by herself. This is a work done within by the Holy Spirit. However, there will always be an outward manifestation of an inward work.

Spiritual Union　　Paul said, "My children, with whom I am again in labor until Christ is formed in you—" (Galatians 4:19). In the physical relationship, a child is formed in a body as a result of the union. In a spiritual relationship, Christ is formed in a body as a result of a believer's union with Jesus Christ.

> Therefore, my brethren, you also were made to die to the Law through the body of Christ, that you might be joined to another, to Him who was raised from the dead, that we might bear fruit for God.
>
> Romans 7:4.

Paul, as the believer joined with Christ, labored in prayer (the King James Version uses "travail") that others might have Christ formed in them. When we are born the first time, we are given physical life. There is life within. When we are born again, the life is formed in us. The life is Jesus Christ. "A new life is begun" (*see* 2 Corinthians 5:17).

Abiding is *not* trying to serve Him, trying to have love, trying to have peace, joy, and so on. It is abiding in Him, keeping His commandments to love others, and being obedient to His will. Then He, the Vine, bears the fruit through us. "So then, you will know them by their fruits" (Matthew 7:20).

This is our beloved Bridegroom, the One who is coming for us. While He is gone, He has given the blessed Holy Spirit to be with each believer everywhere. "And I will pray the Father, and he shall give you another Comforter, that he may abide with you for ever" (John 14:16 KJV).

In Ephesians 5:21–33 we have a beautiful passage on mar-

riage as God planned it. Paul uses a picture of our human relationships as an illustration of Jesus, our Bridegroom, and His
love for us. The marriage illustration seems to be the closest
likeness He can use to describe our relationship to Christ.

In the Bible—the church, the body of believers, is the bride
of Christ. "Husbands, love your wives, just as Christ also loved
the church and gave Himself up for her" (Ephesians 5:25).
Christ is pictured as loving the church—as nourishing and cher-
ishing it, of giving Himself for the bride, and of preparing the
bride to be "holy and without blemish" (*see* v. 27 KJV).

We think of a bride dressed in white—no spots on the dress,
and no wrinkles. This calls for the cleansing of the church and
we are seeing this being done now. Christ uses the hot water
and soap of difficult experiences to remove spots, and a hot iron
—fiery furnace experiences—to remove wrinkles. We also
know: "You are already clean because of the word which I have
spoken to you" (John 15:3). All of this is for Him, in preparation
for meeting Him as His bride. Right in the center of this passage
on marriage He dips from the physical into the spiritual, and
says, "For we are members of his body, of his flesh and of his
bones" (Ephesians 5:30 KJV)—and then goes right back into the
physical relationship of husband and wife (vv. 31–33).

In 1 Corinthians 6:15–20 we once again read a passage teaching truths for the physical relationships. In the middle of this
passage He turns again from the physical to the spiritual. "But
he that is joined unto the Lord is one spirit" (v. 17 KJV)—and
then back into the physical.

The Bride of Christ   I believe that we believers are the bride
of Christ in some mysterious way we do not at all understand.
It is one of those things not as yet revealed. He teaches that we
are one in the Spirit with Him, even as two become one in the
physical union.

Thus we learn: "Now ye are the body of Christ, and members
in particular" (1 Corinthians 12:27 KJV). In this passage we dis-

cover we each have our own place in the body—not all are eyes
or ears or any one part—but we are placed in the body by the
Holy Spirit as He pleases. We are each a part of the body and
Christ is the Head (Ephesians 5:25). It is the head which gives
direction to the physical body. It is the Head—Christ Himself
—which gives direction, nourishment, and care to the spiritual
body—the church—His bride. He encourages men to love their
wives even as Christ loved the church and gave Himself for it.

We are told in Matthew 25:1–13 that the bridesmaids were
waiting for the coming of the Bridegroom. Some were not
ready, and while they went off to prepare, He came, and when
they returned they were too late. We are thus admonished to
be ready—to be watching for Jesus, our Beloved Bridegroom.

He is preparing mansions for us as He waits for the day when
He shall return and take us to be in heaven with Him (John
14:1–6). I believe He is doing all the thoughtful things any
bridegroom would be doing in preparation for the coming of his
bride.

Lessons for Prayer   The study of Jesus as your Saviour and
Bridegroom will greatly affect your prayer life. After a lifetime
of walking with God, Paul said, "That I may know Him, and the
power of His resurrection and the fellowship of His sufferings,
being conformable to His death" (Philippians 3:10).

That I may know Him. Paul's highest goal was not service.
This is a good goal, but not the most important one. To be a good
wife or husband—to be known as a Christian—to provide well
for one's house—these are all good priorities, but Paul had a
higher goal—to know Him.

As you study the life of Christ from the Gospels you will learn
to know Him. You will see His reactions and feel His heartbeat
as He walks with the multitudes. You will walk with Him up the
mountains for quiet communion with the Father. As you pray
to Him, you will learn to listen to Him. As you thank Him for
your salvation, you will hear Him telling you that His death at

the cross completed the sacrifice. As you learn to listen, you will hear Him say He loves you. He does, you know, and nothing can separate you from His love.

As you learn to watch for Jesus Christ, your Bridegroom, you will be excited with the hope that His coming again might be today. Until we see Him and have the marriage supper with Him, we are one in spirit with Him. He is all that we need.

As we pray, learning to know Him more each day, we long for His coming and can say with assurance, "My beloved is mine, and I am his . . ." (Song of Solomon 2:16 KJV).

3

God the Holy Spirit

We have talked together about God the Father and God the Son. Now we want to talk about God the Holy Spirit, the One who brings it all together.

God the Father created the heavens and earth. As a result of the Fall of Adam and Eve (Genesis 3), He sent His Son—Jesus Christ—to earth as a man to redeem the world.

[Know] that you were not redeemed with perishable things like silver or gold from your futile way of life inherited from your forefathers, but with precious blood, as of a lamb unblemished and spotless, the blood of Christ.

1 Peter 1:18, 19

Jesus, my Saviour, paid the price with His life. He rose from the grave and after forty days ascended into heaven where He is now at God's right hand, making intercession for you and me.

And in the same way the Spirit also helps our weakness; for we do not know how to pray as we should, but the Spirit Himself intercedes for us with groanings too deep for words; and He who searches the hearts knows what the mind of the Spirit is, because He intercedes for the saints according to the will of God.

Romans 8:26, 27

While Jesus was on the earth He could only be in one place at a time. He had a human body and, with it, all its limitations. It was necessary that He have that body in order to take our place on the cross.

Because of love, God the Father wanted someone who could be with each believer personally. He wanted someone who would comfort, teach, lead, guide, and generally support the Christian in his own individual needs.

Teacher and Helper   Jesus said, "And I will ask the Father, and He will give you another Helper, that He may be with you forever" (John 14:16).

In verse 17 we read: "Even the Spirit of truth; whom the world cannot receive, because it seeth him not, neither knoweth him: but ye know him; for he dwelleth with you and shall be in you" (KJV).

Those in Satan's cults know that they belong to him. They know that they have made a commitment to Satan, that he dwells within them because they have given their lives to him and he is their master.

Jesus said of the Holy Spirit, the Third Person of the Trinity, that the world can't receive Him because they do not see or know Him. Their eyes are blinded by unbelief, their minds are closed and they really can't see spiritually.

[Jesus says,] "But I tell you the truth, it is to your advantage that I go away; for if I do not go away, the Helper shall not come to you; but if I go, I will send Him to you. And He, when He comes, will convict the world concerning sin, and righteousness, and judgment; concerning sin, because they do not believe in Me; and concerning righteousness, because I go to the Father, and you no longer behold Me; and concerning judgment, because the ruler of this world has been judged. I have many more things to say to you, but you cannot bear them now. But when He, the Spirit of truth, comes, He will guide you into all the truth; for He will not speak on His own initiative, but whatever He hears, He will speak; and He will disclose to you what is to come. He shall glorify Me; for He shall take of Mine, and shall disclose it to you. All things that the Father has are Mine; therefore I said, that He takes of Mine, and will disclose it to you."

John 16:7–15

Jesus said earlier, "If a man love me, he will keep my words: and my Father will love him, and we will come unto him, and make our abode with him" (John 14:23 KJV). He was speaking here of our personal relationship with God.

Luke 24:36–49 is an account of Jesus talking with His disciples after His death. They were afraid of Him because they had seen Him die, and now He was alive right in front of them. He showed them His hands and His feet so that they would believe He was Jesus. They were still afraid, so He asked for something to eat, knowing that eating would make Him seem like one of them. After He ate, He opened their understanding, and then He taught them from the Scriptures. It is still the same today. Our understanding must be opened by God before we can grasp the meaning of Scriptures.

Wait on the Lord   After He taught them, He commissioned them as His witnesses and then said, "And, behold, I send the promise of my Father upon you: but tarry ye in the city of Jerusalem, until ye be endued with power from on high" (Luke 24:49 KJV).

Tarry ye, sit still until you have received power to be the witness I have asked you to be. What a strange command! One would think that with His commissioning there would automatically be power for service, but He disproves this. *Wait!* So many times in the Scriptures we are admonished to wait.

It is difficult for a child to wait. As little ones, we teach the children to wait until the cars have passed before we cross the street. They don't understand. It takes a parent's loving hand to hold them still until it is safe to cross the street. Even as this, it is true with God. We are told in Isaiah to wait on the Lord for strength.

> He gives strength to the weary,
> And to him who lacks might He increases power.
> Though youths grow weary and tired,
> And vigorous young men stumble badly,
> Yet those who wait for the Lord
> Will gain new strength;
> They will mount up with wings like eagles,
> They will run and not get tired,
> They will walk and not become weary.
>
> Isaiah 40:29–31

In Psalms 27:14 KJV we read: "Wait on the Lord: be of good courage, and he shall strengthen thine heart: wait, I say, on the Lord." I believe waiting on God for His timing is one of the hardest things we have to do.

Ruth was told by Naomi: "Sit still, my daughter" (3:18 KJV). It was not yet God's time to move. It was time to sit still. God did more in His own time, as He always does—for when it is in His timing, all the pieces fit together.

We read in the beginning of Acts: "But ye shall receive power, after that the Holy Ghost is come upon you: and ye shall be witnesses unto me both in Jerusalem, and in all Judea, and in Samaria, and unto the uttermost part of the earth" (Acts 1:8 KJV). With this last word of commissioning and promise of the Holy Ghost, Jesus was taken up into the heaven to be at God's right hand. His work here was finished.

They did tarry—and God fulfilled His promise. The Holy

Spirit did come as God had promised and all who witnessed His coming knew He was there in great power. In John 3:8 and Acts 2:2 the Holy Spirit is likened to the wind—we cannot see it, but we are aware of its force. We know where it is and what it has done. We cannot see the Holy Spirit, but we are aware of His power within us. We know when the Word is preached in the power of the Holy Spirit, and when He ministers in the prayer meeting. There is a holy quietness.

God in Us   We believe He—the Holy Spirit—comes in to dwell when we accept Him and give our lives to Christ. The Holy Spirit is God in us—strange, marvelous, and mysterious. We have already seen that Jesus said, "If a man loves me, he will keep my words: and my Father will love him, and we will come unto him, and make our abode with him" (John 14:23 KJV).

There is a witness of the Spirit when God is in us. "The Spirit Himself bears witness with our spirit that we are the children of God" (Romans 8:16). We *do* have new desires, ambitions, and goals. He tells us that we are new creatures in Christ. "Therefore if any man is in Christ, he is a new creature; the old things passed away; behold, new things have come" (2 Corinthians 5:17). When you are born the first time, you enter a physical kingdom. When you are born the second time, you enter a spiritual kingdom.

> Jesus answered, "Truly, truly, I say to you, unless one is born of water and the Spirit, he cannot enter into the kingdom of God. That which is born of the flesh is flesh; and that which is born of the Spirit is spirit."
>
>   John 3:5, 6

The Holy Spirit is within you to be God's will through you. "For it is God who is at work in you, both to will and to work for His good pleasure" (Philippians 2:13).

At this point some people feel that God makes us a mere puppet and, I will confess, Satan tries to tell me this is true. God is *not* the "Big Guy" in the sky who pulls the strings and makes us jump. Remember, God made this planet. He saw Satan lurking in the Garden and He knew he was up to no good. With great heartache, God watched the Fall of this planet. Satan is the "prince of the power of the air" (Ephesians 2:2), a position given him by God until God's time to withdraw that power. God knows where Satan has dug the pits and where he has planted the mines. God knows where the things are that will hurt us and He has given the Holy Spirit to every believer to guide, watch over, comfort, and teach them. "But the Helper, the Holy Spirit, whom the Father will send in My name, He will teach you all things, and bring to your remembrance all that I said to you" (John 14:26).

No, God does not pull the strings. He has given us a free will and we can let Him *lead* us through this maze, or we can keep our lives in our own hands and go blundering through. We can quench the Spirit and ignore Him if we wish. The decision is ours. (*see* 1 Thessalonians 5:19–22).

God is Light (Psalms 27:1) and as He walks with us there is Light around us. The Bible says: "Thy word is a lamp unto my feet, and a light unto my path" (Psalms 119:105 KJV). And from the Living Bible: "Your words are a flashlight to light the path ahead of me, and keep me from stumbling."

I remember walking to the college across a dark field from a house near Westmont. Someone kindly shone a light on my feet. It was dark all around me, but light at my feet. This is a beautiful picture of God's guidance and protection. I could see clearly where to step.

As the Holy Spirit lives God's life in us, He does not make us blobs! We are personalities. God made us this way. The Holy Spirit magnifies God through us.

I will give thanks to Thee, for I am fearfully and
    wonderfully made;
Wonderful are Thy works,
And my soul knows it very well.
My frame was not hidden from Thee,
When I was made in secret,
And skillfully wrought in the depths of the earth.
Thine eyes have seen my unformed substance;
And in Thy book they were all written,
The days that were ordained for me,
When as yet there was not one of them.
How precious also are Thy thoughts to me, O God!
How vast is the sum of them!

                                                        Psalms 139:14–17

Fruit of the Spirit   The fruit of the Spirit is listed for us in
Galatians. Fruit is usually borne on a fruit tree—the tree faithfully reproducing its own kind. "For each tree is known by its
own fruit. For men do not gather figs from thorns, nor do they
pick grapes from a briar bush" (Luke 6:44). In this passage God
uses this illustration to explain to us the working of the Holy
Spirit within us. Fruit is automatically borne on the tree—it is
a *result.* The spiritual fruit listed in Galatians 5 is also a result. They are listed as love, joy, peace, longsuffering, gentleness, goodness, faith, meekness, and temperance (*see* vv. 22,
23 KJV). These are the direct results of the Holy Spirit's presence.

The Holy Spirit—God in us—is just as much a part of the
Trinity as God the Father and God the Son. None is lifted higher
than the other—they are all One. Each has His own particular
work to do, but They are equal.

Our attitude toward the Trinity—God the Father, God the
Son, and God the Holy Spirit—greatly affects our prayer life. It

is important that we submit to Him and let Him direct. As the Holy Spirit—the Teacher—teaches us about the Trinity, and as we seek to know Jesus, we will find new plateaus of prayer and will grow in our knowledge of Him.

4

The School of Prayer

"I have prayed, and I prayed with His faith and things are getting worse!"

Cal and I have heard this many times and we have gone through this experience ourselves. I recall a man in a Bible-study group many years ago asking me if I felt there was any prayer life beyond "If it be Thy will." I had a need to feel adequate and I said *no*. It was such a pat answer.

In John 14:12 we read (and Jesus is speaking): "Truly, truly, I say to you, he who believes in Me, the works that I do shall he do also; and greater works than these shall he do; because I go to the Father." A beautiful prayer promise follows: "And whatever you ask in My name, that will I do, that the Father may be glorified in the Son. If you ask Me anything in My name, I will do it. If you love Me, you will keep My commandments" (vv. 13–15). How well I remember the first time I really heard these verses. They were read at a conference by a returned missionary from China. She told how some of the Chinese young people had caught the vision of that verse and of the prayer promise following. She shared some of the miracles that had come as a result of their believing prayers. It was as if God had sent her to me. The Holy Spirit wrote her words across my heart. It is true that I was seeking light on the subject of prayer, but taking this verse literally seemed so presumptuous. I decided to leave it alone.

God had been speaking to me on the subject of prayer. The

Holy Spirit was faithfully using the question the man had asked me, "Do you feel there is any prayer life beyond 'If it be Thy will'?" I was testing God.

I decided one time to see if fasting and prayer really worked. It was near payday, but our cupboard wasn't really empty. I decided to test God, and I fasted and prayed, asking for groceries! How patient God is. Of course the groceries didn't come— it is God's will that we have groceries. "Do not be anxious then, saying, 'What shall we eat?' or 'What shall we drink?' or 'With what shall we clothe ourselves?' For all these things the Gentiles eagerly seek; for your heavenly Father knows that you need all these things. But seek first His kingdom, and His righteousness; and all these things shall be added to you" (Matthew 6:31–33). And in Luke: ". . . . For behold, the kingdom of God is in your midst [or within you]" (17:21). God is dwelling within when we have accepted Him. As we believe, what we eat, drink, and wear are His concern. They will be given.

When we fast and it is scriptural, we fast because we have a burden from God for a soul or for something for which He wants us deeply concerned. As we are in Christ in prayer, His business becomes our concern and our business becomes His! Exciting! And it lifts the load.

That was just one of the many mistakes I've made in prayer. It was some time before I realized why God hadn't answered that day. He gave me the desire to keep trying. I know any desire to pray is from Him. There were desperate needs. We had to have answers, so we kept reading and praying.

"Teach Us to Pray"   The disciples were gathered around Jesus one day. As He prayed with them, they had noticed His prayers to His Father were different from theirs. One of them asked Him to teach them to pray as John the Baptist taught his disciples (Luke 11:1).

"Lord, teach us to pray!" This is the heart-cry of many today. There is heartache and difficulty everywhere. The disciples went to the right source. Only God can teach us *to* pray and *how* to pray.

Prayer is talking—prayer is communication. Prayer is getting into communion with God. We communicate in many ways besides talking. We communicate with body language—the way we use our hands, the way we eat, sit, stand, and walk. The language we use, the tone of our voices, and the look on our faces all reveal much about our real selves. All that we do reveals the true self.

We hear much about positive and negative attitudes today. We know that as we expect positive results, we receive them. This is akin to behavioral psychology, and God taught it centuries ago. Solomon, one of the wisest men who ever lived, said, "For as he thinks within himself, so he is . . ." (Proverbs 23:7). We actually bring to pass that which we believe will come to pass. "For what I fear comes upon me, And what I dread befalls me" (Job 3:25).

The prayer promises in the Word are positive. "Ask, and it shall be given to you; seek, and you shall find; knock, and it shall be opened to you. For every one who asks receives, and he who seeks finds, and to him who knocks it shall be opened" (Matthew 7:7, 8). A definite request—a definite answer.

In Jeremiah we read: "Call to Me, and I will answer you, and I will tell you great and mighty things, which you do not know" (33:3). *You call, and I will answer.* Very positive.

Jesus says: "And whatever you ask in My name, that will I do, that the Father may be glorified in the Son. If you ask Me anything in My name, I will do it" (John 14:13, 14).

These are positive statements from Jesus Himself. You probably have asked many times, as I have, "Why, then, don't we see answers?"

If we want any relationship to be good, we have to keep open and honest. We have to be truthful about things we don't understand and the things that bother us. We have to work on it each day. God calls for this same honesty. He calls us away from playing Christian games and Christian role playing. He calls us away from praying by rote and from praying to Him from a sheltered place—traditional prayers and surroundings.

Belief Is Positive   He speaks to us with a positive voice, calling us from the negative things that hinder His answers.

> Be anxious for nothing, but in everything by prayer and supplication with thanksgiving let your requests be made known to God. And the peace of God, which surpasses all comprehension, shall guard your hearts and your minds in Christ Jesus.
>
> Philippians 4:6, 7

In the human area, being anxious brings an uneasy feeling that things are not going right. We feel we need to do something about it. This is a do-it-yourself world. We are made to feel we are weak if we need others' help—even help from other Christians.

Anxiety is negative. Anxiety is worry. Worry is sin. Will sin affect your answers to prayer? "We ought to pray and not to lose heart" (*see* Luke 18:1). To lose heart means to become discouraged—to give up before one sees the answer. To give up before the answer comes is unbelief. Unbelief is negative. Unbelief is sin.

Peter is told: "Keep watching and praying, that you may not enter into temptation; the spirit is willing, but the flesh is weak" (Matthew 26:41). Jesus was praying in the Garden. This was His night of supreme agony and grief. He took Peter, James, and John with Him. Jesus also needed others near in His time of crisis. He states a positive fact—*the spirit is willing . . . the flesh is weak*. This could be the reason so many of us have prayerless lives even though we love our Saviour to the best of our ability. Prayer takes time and much energy. *The spirit is willing . . . the flesh is weak.* To allow the flesh to dominate the spirit life is putting self before God. Self before God is negative. Self before God is sin.

In the Epistles we are told to pray with thanksgiving (*see* Colossians 4:2; Philippians 4:6). Giving thanks *before* we see the answer is faith—positive belief is an attitude toward God. Again we are asked to pray with thanksgiving and without anger and resentment: "First of all, then, I urge that entreaties and prayers, petitions and thanksgivings, be made on behalf of all men. . . . Therefore I want the men in every place to pray, lifting up holy hands, without wrath and dissension" (1 Timothy 2:1, 8). Thanksgiving is praise to God—a thankful heart, a positive attitude. Anger and resentment are negative attitudes and God says that they are sin. The two attitudes of thanksgiving and resentful anger cannot coexist. Anger, not dealt with, gives Satan a foothold in a life—a place to enter in and deceive. "And do not give the devil an opportunity" (Ephesians 4:27).

In Christ there will be indignation that will bring a course of action. This is feeling under God's control, not anger fed by Satan. Jesus was indignant when He saw the money changers in the temple. The attitude brought action—He drove them out. I hope you would have a like feeling if you saw a Bible being burned or the American flag trampled underfoot. I trust you would do something about it.

Self and all its fruits are negative attitudes and bring negative results. God says to believe that you have them and you shall. Ask, believing with single-mindedness—not double-mindedness. A double-minded person does not know his own mind. He does not really ask. He doesn't know what to ask for. If we do not know our own minds, these negative attitudes block God's answers from us.

Confess Your Sins   The Psalmist David said, "If I regard wickedness in my heart, the Lord will not hear" (Psalms 66:18). Wickedness has to do with self, doing things our own way—

reaping the results of our decisions.

"If we confess our sins, He is faithful and righteous to forgive us our sins and to cleanse us from all unrighteousness" (1 John 1:9). I do believe this verse is God's spiritual therapy for today. I know the price was paid on the cross for my sin. Thank You, Father! However, we need to name the sin we have committed. We need to face it—to say it—so that we will remember later, when Satan tries to smear us with false guilt, that we did name it. We need to remember we put it under the Blood! This is the place of cleansing. Real guilt is guilt in an area not yet confessed. False guilt is Satan accusing us in an area already cleansed. We need to accept, along with God's gift of cleansing, His gift of forgiveness for others and ourselves—lest we be caught up in bitterness and resentment.

We are to pray *at all times* (Ephesians 6:18), and to pray *without ceasing* (1 Thessalonians 5:17). It isn't practical to believe that we should be on our knees or reading our Bibles all the time. This was not the life of Jesus as He walked on the earth. It is, instead, an attitude. Jesus healed the sick, fed the hungry, washed the disciples' feet, and did so many other things. He said He came to serve, but His mind was on the Father as He served. He came to do the Father's will and He kept His mind on Him that He might always be in His will.

We read in Psalms: "Cease striving and know that I am God ..." (46:10). God says, "Be still," which is a definite act (KJV). In Isaiah we read: "Thou wilt keep him in perfect peace, whose mind is stayed [or placed] on thee ..." (26:3 KJV). Again:

> He gives strength to the weary,
> And to him who lacks might He increases power.
> Though youths grow weary and tired,
> And vigorous young men stumble badly,
> Yet those who wait for the Lord
> Will gain new strength;

They will mount up with wings like eagles,
They will run and not get tired,
They will walk and not become weary.

Isaiah 40:29–31

No one has pat answers for prayer. The disciples said, "Teach us to pray." It is a school and we can trust the Holy Spirit to teach us. He is the Teacher. "But the Helper, the Holy Spirit, whom the Father will send in My name, He will teach you all things, and bring to your remembrance all that I said to you" (John 14:26). Also, we know that we are temples of the Holy Spirit: "Or do you not know that your body is a temple of the Holy Spirit who is in you, whom you have from God, and that you are not your own?" (1 Corinthians 6:19). People go to a temple to pray. The Holy Spirit prays through us as our hearts fellowship with His.

I believe that when a person comes to your mind again and again, the Holy Spirit is praying through you according to that person's need. He may be many miles away, but God hears and answers. We are simply the vessel used. I believe that the Holy Spirit takes our heart-agony to God in prayer (*see* Romans 8:27). He puts it into the words we cannot express. Sometimes we cannot bring it into focus enough to pray for it. He—the Holy Spirit—does it for us!

Prayer Attitudes   We may, as we pour out our hearts to God, wonder if our physical position during prayer is correct. The Scripture has quite a bit to say about posture, but there is no definite position which God prefers.

King Solomon stood and spread his hands to God (1 Kings 8:22), and also knelt before God in the presence of all the assembly spreading forth his hands toward heaven (2 Chronicles 6:*). Both times were for prayers of dedication.

The Psalmist David lifted his hands (Psalms 28:2), prayed while kneeling (Psalms 95:6), and David and his elders were "on their faces" before God (1 Chronicles 21:16).

The Israelites fell on their faces before God, because of sin among them (Numbers 16:22). Joshua is pictured on his face before a heavenly messenger (Joshua 5:14).

We read of Jesus on His face before God in the Garden (Matthew 26:39). Jesus refers to believers praying as they stand (Mark 11:25), and (in 1 Timothy 2:8) believers are encouraged to lift up holy hands.

Paul knelt before God (Acts 20:36), as did Daniel three times a day (Daniel 6:10).

Before God, it is the attitude of heart that matters. "Man looks on the outward appearance but God looks on the heart" (*see* 1 Samuel 16:7). God does see the heart—whether it is sincere or playing a role of prayer. Pious phrases, acts of worship, attitudes of prayer, and positions of prayer are all a game if there is not honest communication and communion. In Luke we have a classic example of prayer from God's viewpoint and ours:

> And He also told this parable to certain ones who trusted in themselves that they were righteous, and viewed others with contempt: "Two men went up into the temple to pray, one a Pharisee, and the other a tax-gatherer. The Pharisee stood and was praying thus to himself, 'God, I thank Thee that I am not like other people: swindlers, unjust, adulterers, or even like this tax-gatherer. I fast twice a week; I pay tithes of all that I get.'
>
> "But the tax-gatherer, standing some distance away, was even unwilling to lift up his eyes to heaven, but was beating his breast, saying, 'God, be merciful to me, the sinner!'
>
> "I tell you, this man went down to his house justified rather than the other; for every one who exalts himself shall be humbled, and he who humbles himself shall be exalted."
>
> Luke 18:9–14

When we list for God the sins we do *not* commit, we have a problem. This is pride! When we have to thank God that we are not sinners like someone else present—we are not honest with ourselves or God. We are all sinners. I believe that the only time He lets us see someone's sin is so that we might pray for the sinner—not to talk about it. This is "closet prayer." It should never be given as a prayer request. It is different if a person wants to share his own problem in body-life. Even here there needs to be Holy Spirit discernment. When we have a need to push someone else down so that we might look better, we have a problem.

Prayer is fellowship—heart-to-heart communion. As we level with God about our hurts and needs, He shows us how to pray for others and their problems.

God says there must be forgiveness: "For if you forgive men for their transgressions, your heavenly Father will also forgive you. But if you do not forgive men, then your Father will not forgive your transgressions" (Matthew 6:14, 15). We are reminded that some have been *so* hurt and have known so much rejection. You can't really pray for the one who hurt you until you take your own hurts to God and let Him heal them. The very real rejection and resulting resentments and bitterness must be taken care of first. Sometimes we battle in prayer. At other times we must take time to rest in God. He wants us to sit quietly and let Him tell us He loves us. As we listen, He will tell us that we are precious and He knows our heartache. He will heal our hurts.

Stay close beside Him until your restless soul is calm. "Come to Me, all who are weary and heavy-laden, and I will give you rest. Take My yoke upon you, and learn from Me, for I am gentle and humble in heart; and you shall find rest for your souls. For My yoke is easy, and My load is light" (Matthew 11:28–30). "Just as the Father has loved Me, I have also loved you; abide in My love" (John 15:9).

Take a Friend to Jesus   *Abide* means "Please feel at home, sit down, take off your shoes and rest awhile." As He eases your heartache, you can trust Him to deal gently with areas of forgiveness that may need to be dealt with. When you and I try to walk with a friend over a rough spot, we cannot reach the hurt. When Jesus Himself does it, His love surrounds and fills us. "And hope does not disappoint, because the love of God has been poured out within our hearts through the Holy Spirit who was given to us" (Romans 5:5). He does the work. No one understands exactly what another is going through. To say we understand is a pat answer. God alone understands and, as we take our friends to Him, He heals.

I'm reminded of the four who took their friend to Jesus:

And many were gathered together, so that there was no longer room, even near the door; and He was speaking the word to them. And they came, bringing to Him a paralytic, carried by four men. And being unable to get to Him on account of the crowd, they removed the roof above Him; and when they had dug an opening, they let down the pallet on which the paralytic was lying.

And Jesus seeing their faith said to the paralytic, "My son, your sins are forgiven." But there were some of the scribes sitting there and reasoning in their hearts, "Why does this man speak that way? He is blaspheming; who can forgive sins but God alone?"

And immediately Jesus, perceiving in His spirit that they were reasoning that way within themselves, said to them, "Why are you reasoning about these things in your hearts? Which is easier, to say to the paralytic, 'Your sins are forgiven'; or to say, 'Arise, and take up your pallet and walk'? But in order that you may know that the Son of Man has authority on earth to forgive sins," He said to the paralytic, "I say to you, rise, take up your pallet and go home." And he rose and immediately took up the pallet and went out in the sight of all; so that they were all amazed and were glorifying God, saying, "We have never seen anything like this."

Mark 2:2–12

The house was so full that they couldn't get in. These men were not defeated by all of the obstacles in their way. They took their friend to the roof, made a hole large enough to let the stretcher through, and lowered him to rest at Jesus' feet.

What an unusual way for people to take a friend to Jesus! Did it cost the four friends anything? Indeed it did! It cost them time and effort to take him there. It also cost them money to repair the roof. Was it worth it? It surely was—their friend *walked* away. It is always worthwhile to take a friend to Jesus.

Job saw his trials finally break when he prayed for his friends. "And the Lord restored the fortunes of Job when he prayed for his friends, and the Lord increased all that Job had twofold" (Job 42:10).

5

Faith and Trust

"I really need help," Mary said as she played with the handle of her purse. Then she lifted her head and looked at me. "Jim, our eighteen-year-old, is lying to me. I can't trust him."

"I can't trust him." How often we hear that today. Trust is the very basis of a good relationship. Without it, we may want to believe, we may try to believe, but deep within our hearts we doubt. We doubt the person and his words.

Mary and her husband, Pete, had had some difficult times in their marriage. Both of them knew and loved the Lord. However, Pete found it hard to be completely honest with Mary. Each time they made up after an argument, Mary found it harder to believe him—and now seeing his patterns in their son filled her with resentment. It all seemed so hopeless.

As we talked together, I asked Mary about her mother-father relationships. She told me a familiar story. Her own father had not really been a father to her. He would promise to take her somewhere and then fail to keep his word. She could not remember him taking her on his lap or holding her in his arms. When she was twelve he left with another woman. She had to take care of her younger brothers and sisters while her mother worked to support the family.

Mary's trust had been broken. As Mary had been programmed by circumstances, so are we all programmed by our experiences. Mary was taught by her father (not intentionally) that she could not trust people—that they would not keep their word.

As we talked, Mary discovered that she had no real basis for trusting people—she had been shown little pattern for trust. Through the training of her childhood, she had learned not to trust. She was surprised to find out that she didn't trust her husband—that she had no pattern to trust men. It affected her attitude toward all men, including her son. "For as he thinketh in his heart, so is he . . ." (Proverbs 23:7 KJV). We are what we think—not what we think we are. People around us pick up our attitudes—our vibrations—those things we think we have hidden. Subconsciously, Mary was revealing that she didn't trust men. We reap what we sow (Galatians 6:7), and the attitude which she had revealed to others came back to her.

Mary's trust needed to be healed. Her trust was a part of her mind programming. The mind is in the soul. David said, "Heal my soul" (Psalms 41:4) and, "He restoreth my soul . . ." (Psalms 23:3 KJV). For the Psalmist, something had been broken and restored. It is God Himself who does the healing, the restoring.

Mary and I discussed the fact that <u>we need a pattern</u>—that <u>we need to know how to do something</u> before we can do it. We discussed the fact that we must have a pattern for a certain kind of dress if we want it to come out correctly. We must have a recipe for what we want to cook if we want it to turn out as it should. I know that some women say they never use a recipe —that they just take a pinch of this and a shake of that. Either someone taught them or they learned by themselves through practice. We know what bread is like without yeast or leavening. One is not born knowing how to read, to type, or to drive a car. A baby does not learn to smile unless he sees smiles, nor does he learn to laugh unless he hears laughter. We are born mimics! That is why babies in Spanish-speaking homes speak Spanish and in French-speaking homes, speak French. We are taught by our parents and those near us.

Mary asked me to pray for God to heal her trust. *Heal my soul.* When it is broken in one area, it is hurt in all areas. Her trust in men, women, and herself was all damaged. The main area we prayed about was her trust in God.

A Pattern for Trust   We see God, our Father, in the same pattern in which trust has been programmed by an earthly father. We want to trust God, we try to trust Him, we attempt to put full faith in Him, but somehow it doesn't seem real. We are trying, but getting nowhere.

The same can be true with a husband or wife. When we have been programmed not to trust men or women—when we could not trust a mother or a father—we find it difficult to really trust a mate. We will try to trust him, we will say we trust him, but we may have a need to police or possess him. There will be a need to know where the husband or wife is, and what he is doing. That shows lack of trust.

I know a young girl whose father deliberately taught her not to trust. When she was small, he sat her on top of a wall and had her jump into his arms. He did this three consecutive times. The fourth time he had her jump from the wall, but didn't catch her —he let her fall. The father told her this was to teach her not to trust men. You can imagine her difficulties. This incident has affected every area of her life. She has difficulty talking to God, her Father.

As Mary and I prayed, we prayed for God to heal her trust in Him, in men, in women, and in herself. Trusting yourself is self-confidence, affecting your performance at every level. Since this time, Mary has seen much healing. With her trust being healed, Mary is beginning to relax. As she learns to trust, both her husband, Pete, and her son, Jim, are showing her more trust and respect in return.

We must not discuss something our parents have done in order to be critical of them. We should only state facts, that we might pray about them. We are told in Matthew 7:1 that we are not to judge—and we dare not! God will judge them, and He will also judge *us* for our attitudes. We are to forgive, and forgiveness, like trust, will come back. True forgiveness always comes from God. When *we* forgive, the hurt may come back later to clobber us. When we accept God's forgiveness for someone, some situation, or ourselves, it is forgiven. We can remember it, but the hurt is gone.

In Psalms we read about some definite keys in the Christian's walk and prayer life.

> Trust in the Lord, and do good. . . .
> And He will give you the desires of your heart.
> Commit your way to the Lord,
> Trust also in Him, and He will do it.
>
> Psalms 37:3–5

We are told to trust in the Lord and to do good—two positive actions. To *trust* is the opposite of *to be afraid*. To trust is the opposite of living in the fears that would bind us and enslave us if they were allowed.

The result of this trust in the Lord is the healing, surging flow of power through us—the power of the Holy Spirit. He cuts us loose from the very fears that would paralyze all life within us, keeping us tied to the crutches of hopelessness and despair.

Trust in the Lord brings the positive action of doing good. Each attitude brings results. *Doing good* is a positive action that brings good results in others' lives.

> [Peter said:] "You know of Jesus of Nazareth, how God anointed Him with the Holy Spirit and with power, and how He went about doing good, and healing all who were oppressed by the devil: for God was with Him."
>
> Acts 10:38

And be kind to one another, tender-hearted, forgiving each other, just as God in Christ also has forgiven you.

> Ephesians 4:32

Love is patient, love is kind and is not jealous; love does not brag and is not arrogant.

1 Corinthians 13:4

To sum up, let all be harmonious, sympathetic, brotherly, kindhearted, and humble in spirit.

1 Peter 3:8

[Jesus said:] "For if you forgive men for their transgressions, your heavenly Father will also forgive you."

Matthew 6:14

But whom you forgive anything, I forgive also; for indeed what I have forgiven, if I have forgiven anything, I did it for your sakes in the presence of Christ.

2 Corinthians 2:10

These are positive attitudes and actions of good. As we trust in Him and do good, we shall dwell in His land and be fed.

Christ the Servant   I love the scene on the beach where the disciples had gone fishing after Christ's death and Resurrection, as recorded in John 21. Jesus was gone and they had gone back to their fishing. They had fished all night and hadn't caught anything. How discouraging!

At dawn they saw a man on the shore who called to them to ask if they had caught anything. They told him *no* and then He did a strange thing. He told them where to put down the net to find fish. How foolish! For some reason, they obeyed. As a result of this obedience, they reaped much reward—a net full of fish (money) and renewed faith. Their faith had been severely tried by their own lack of trust as they walked far from Christ in His time of trial. The night of darkness had revealed to them their own lack of ability to follow Christ as they wanted to. They were hurt over their own lack of commitment in following Him. I believe that in going back to something they had done before (fishing), they were trying to find the security of the familiar, because His reassuring presence was gone. When one we love is gone, we try to fill the loneliness with other identifications. We do try to go back to the familiar—friends, job, town, and so on.

With the large catch, Peter's spiritual eyes were opened and he knew the Man on shore was his Lord. I'm touched by his exuberance as he plunged into the water and swam ashore. He wasn't interested in waiting for the others to get the fish into the boat and the boat to land.

The Lord served the men fish and bread. There was a fire built and He had prepared the food. He also served it! This is a beautiful picture of Jesus—the Servant. In John 13 He took a towel and washed the disciples' feet, gently drying them. He did not ask one of them to do it. He did it Himself. He set an example for us in service. The closer one is to Christ, the more he is able to serve. We read: ". . . . I am among you as the one who serves" (Luke 22:27).

Trust in the Lord, and do good. We will serve and the service will be done for Christ and not for others. "Whatever you do, do your work heartily, as for the Lord rather than for men; knowing that from the Lord you will receive the reward of the inheritance. It is the Lord Christ whom you serve" (Colossians 3:23, 24).

. . . so shalt thou dwell in the land [with Him], and verily thou shalt be fed [by Him].

Psalms 37:3 KJV

Thou dost prepare a table before me in the presence of my enemies; Thou hast anointed my head with oil. . . .

Psalms 23:5

These are two beautiful pictures of Christ serving us. In the first He is the Servant preparing the food for each of us personally—individual service. And, "in the presence of my enemies," Jesus—my Saviour and Bridegroom—is taking care of me right in front of everyone. He is taking care of me when my enemies are all around. With Him there, preparing for me and serving me, what else matters? His Holy Presence is Light in the midst!

The second picture reveals Christ serving as my High Priest —the one who goes into the Holy of Holies to intercede with God on my behalf! (Hebrews 4:14–16). It was the High Priest who did the anointing. *Thou [Christ] hast anointed my head with oil.* Oil here means the Holy Spirit. The head was anointed, the oil ran down. In this case even the cup was full to overflowing. No wonder he (David) could know that the positive actions of "goodness and lovingkindness" would follow him all of his life, with the promise of life forever with Christ (Psalms 23:6).

Commitment and Cleansing   We read: "Delight yourself in the Lord" (Psalms 37:4), and we realize—as we view David's Christ as pictured in Psalm 23—the loveliness of Christ. As much as we try to delight in Him, we never achieve the attitude of delight which we wish we had. He, the Holy Spirit within, delights in God through us. As we submit to Him and allow the Spirit to minister through us, He will give us our hearts' desires. In the process of learning to allow Him to do this, our desires are cleansed and purified. He loves to give us the desires of our hearts. One in this position knows the opening, giving hand of God.

Again: "Commit your way to the Lord . . ." (Psalms 37:5). *Commit* means to turn something over—to let go of it. Then, in the same verse: ". . . Trust also in Him, and He will do it."

When a child is two or three he may insist on trying to tie his shoelaces. He is not old enough to be taught that particular thing, but just old enough to be stubborn and say, "I want to do it myself." Sometimes we have to deliberately take the laces out of his hands and tie them for him.

Later on we teach him, step by step, holding his little hands in ours, as we tie the laces together. What a picture of God—taking things we won't commit and doing them Himself. He longs to teach us, and as we submit our hands and lives to Him, He does it with great patience!

Many times there is a situation we have worked on and prayed over, only to have it remain broken. He says to commit and trust. Lay it down—hands off—He will do it. May God give us grace to let the Holy Spirit trust God through us! Sometimes the trust pattern is so broken that we have to let the Holy Spirit trust God through us. This is a position of surrender. (*See* Galatians 5:22, 23 on the work of the Spirit.)

Faith and *trust* are used interchangeably in Scripture. The condition of your trust, whether or not it has been broken, will greatly affect your faith—and your faith will affect your prayer life.

"Now faith is the substance of things hoped for, the evidence of things not seen" (Hebrews 11:1 KJV). "But without faith it is impossible to please [God]: for he that cometh to God must believe that he is, and that he is a rewarder of them that diligently seek him" (v. 6 KJV).

Most of us want to please God, and we try to please Him, but go away from His presence feeling we haven't pleased Him. If we are to be very honest, we are not pleased with our prayer fellowship with Him. In fact, at a still deeper level of honesty, many of us are not pleased with God. We feel He is asking the impossible, that life has been one failure after another, so why should we try God anymore?

We who have been hurt in mother-father relationships are in this position. We have tried and tried to please a parent or someone else, and have never succeeded. We feel we have never pleased God. We think He sees us as we see ourselves— one failure after another.

One of the times I felt God's presence near was the time I

really saw Galatians 2:20. Sometimes we merely read, and sometimes we see. I had been looking at my faith. (That was part of the problem. I was looking at *myself*.) My faith was so thin and shallow. It was so full of holes, and the situation called for strong faith.

Suddenly the Holy Spirit spoke to me: "I have been crucified with Christ; and it is no longer I who live, but Christ lives in me; and the life which I now live in the flesh I live by faith [of] the Son of God, who loved me, and delivered Himself up for me" (Galatians 2:20). These are the words that became alive (*see* King James Version): "I live by the faith of the Son of God, who loved me, and gave himself for me."—*I live by His faith.* God confirmed it with Galatians 5:22, 23 where the fruit of the Spirit is listed—the fruit being the attributes of God lived through us by Him. His faith is one of them and is a result of my relationship with Him. Romans 12:3 tells us that each believer is given a measure of faith. "So then faith cometh by hearing, and hearing by the word of God" (Romans 10:17 KJV). The faithfulness of God is programmed in as we read. Faith is strengthened as it is used.

Suppose Queen Elizabeth wrote to you personally and told you to present her letter at the gates of her palace. The guards were to let you in; you could eat at her table, wear clothing from the palace, and go into any room you desired. It would take a great deal of faith and trust in her for you to go. You would probably present the letter timidly—I know I would. At the proper time, the gates would swing open and you would be welcome. Every promise would be kept. For an added benefit, she would have you keep the letter and ask you to come again anytime. The next time you would not be as timid! Your previous experience would have given you confidence.

The Substance of Faith   We can know faith in a person and trust in his word. This is the very essence of prayer. God said, "Come, ask, and I will keep My promises" (*see* Matthew 7:7, 8).

Ask, and it shall be given you; seek, and ye shall find;
knock and it shall be opened unto you: For every one that
asketh receiveth; and he that seeketh findeth; and to him
that knocketh it shall be opened.

Matthew 7:7, 8 KJV

Remember, we pray with His faith.

Faith is substance. Substance is something real.

Faith is evidence. Evidence is so real that it is used in court
to prove a case.

Faith is the substance of things hoped for. Ask for those
things you hope for.

The evidence of things not seen. Ask for this evidence—that
the things your eye only sees by faith will become a reality.

David said, "When I am afraid, I will put my trust in Thee"
(Psalms 56:3). This is a deliberate act—taking our eyes off the
thing we fear, taking our eyes off our own ability to do anything,
and trusting God to do everything.

Jesus said: ". . . apart from Me you can do nothing" (John 15:5).
He gave us another verse to balance that one: "I can do all
things through Him who strengthens me" (Philippians 4:13).
These two verses are needed together. We have been taught
that we are unworthy, and we beat ourselves down. We were
unworthy for salvation, but never worthless. Ephesians 2:1–10
tells us that even when we were dead in sins, Christ died for us.
What love! In Christ we are very worthy and can do all things.
I do not understand this. I am only grateful for it. Only the Holy
Spirit can make this truth real to us.

Our attitude toward ourselves—our feeling of failure *or* our
trust in Him—will greatly affect our prayer lives. Some people
go to Him timidly, feeling insignificant and broken, crawling
into His presence and afraid to ask. We are in Him; He is our
Righteousness. "But by His doing you are in Christ Jesus, who
became to us wisdom from God, and righteousness and sanctifi-

cation, and redemption" (1 Corinthians 1:30). We are told to come confidently: "Let us therefore draw near with confidence to the throne of grace, that we may receive mercy and may find grace to help in time of need" (Hebrews 4:16).

Daniel's Faith Rewarded   Daniel trusted in God and placed his faith there as he prayed. (*See* Daniel 6:10.) He knew men were conniving to have him killed. Nevertheless, he calmly kept his schedule. He opened the window as usual. His faith was in God. Were there results? Yes, there were. We always live with the results of a decision. If he had not continued his prayer life, or if he had prayed silently with windows closed, he would have had to live with the results of that decision.

The results were that Daniel ended up in the lions' den. The lions' dinner was not Daniel, but those who had plotted to have him killed. God had closed the lions' mouths. The king himself came to check on Daniel the next morning and commanded the others to be thrown in. Daniel's faith was in God, not men (vv. 11–28).

Abraham's Trustful Faith   Abraham is another marvelous example of faith. He followed God from his own land to a strange land, not knowing where he was going (Hebrews 11:8). He only knew that God was leading.

His faith in God and His mercy, as he prayed for the people of Lot's city, showed the depth of his compassion and trust (Genesis 18:23–33).

In Genesis 22 Abraham's faith shone as he obeyed God in the instructions to sacrifice his son Isaac. Isaac's birth was a miracle given to Abraham by God. Abraham knew that if Isaac's life was taken, ". . . God was able to raise him up, even from the dead; from whence also he received him in a figure" (Hebrews 11:19 KJV). God did provide a substitute sacrifice that day, as He does for us in Christ.

Abraham had lapses of faith. He told Sarah to tell King

Abimelech that she was his sister. He was afraid for his life. (*See* Genesis 20.) God is good to let us see the weak areas of His people, for they encourage us.

Abraham's son Isaac did exactly the same thing as his father (Genesis 26:7). We *do* pattern our children!

It reveals the love and mercy of God that Abraham is not remembered for his failures, but for his faith. ". . . And Abraham believed God, and it was reckoned to him as righteousness" (Romans 4:3). Abraham counted God faithful.

Noah's Focus on God   Noah's faith was beautiful as it shone against the darkness of the sin of his day. How seemingly stupid was God's request to build a big boat in a desert area! And remember—it had not rained up to this time. Noah's eye focused on God as he steadfastly did exactly what God told him to do. It must have been difficult, humanly speaking, to have his neighbors jeer at him, "How's your boat coming, Noah?"

I wonder what his wife said to him about this boat! It would have kept him away from home a great deal, and probably ran up a big bill at the lumber company. I wonder what his sons said to him about this unusual invention. I wonder how they took the laughter and jokes of other young people. It is often hard for children to hear their fathers ridiculed.

Do you realize that they had to enter the boat before it started to rain? I can see the people crowding around, watching and joking as the animals went on board. I'm so grateful for Genesis 6:22: "Thus Noah did; according to all that God had commanded him, so he did." Do you suppose Noah ever dreamed that centuries later other believers, such as we, would be grateful that he trusted God and put his faith in Him? Noah saw with the eye of faith. The Scripture bears out that he was the head of his home and had trained his children well. They went into the ark with him. God had provided wives for his three sons from that godless civilization! God is faithful.

This recalls a favorite story of mine. In one of my children's

Sunday-school classes, I taught the names of Noah's three sons: Ham, Shem, and Japheth. I asked a small girl to repeat them for me and she said, "Ham, Spam, and Japheth." Whether it was Shem or Spam didn't make much difference that long-ago day. He and his wife went in with the others and their lives were saved.

The Bible says, ". . . the Lord shut him in" (Genesis 7:16 KJV). God shut the door. I imagine Noah and his family would have been tempted to let neighbors in after it started to rain, but God shut the door. The time for deciding to believe was past.

Lot's Failure   How opposite is the story of Lot, Abraham's nephew. Lot was a believer—"For by what he saw and heard that righteous man, while living among them, felt his righteous soul tormented day after day with their lawless deeds" (*see* 2 Peter 2:8). The Bible refers to him as a righteous man.

But Lot's decisions were never of faith. Lot was always number one! He wanted the best property, even though it meant living and rearing his family among a godless society (Genesis 13:10–13).

When it was time for that city to be destroyed because of its wickedness, God had to tell Abraham. He couldn't even tell Lot since his ears were not tuned into God. They were tuned into the world. Lot tried to take his daughters' fiancés with him. They wouldn't believe him when he warned them that the city would be destroyed—they only laughed at him. His wife and two single daughters did leave with him, but his wife was so broken up over leaving her wealth, friends, and "things" that she looked back for one last glance and turned into a pillar of salt. God had told them *not* to look back.

The story of Lot's life ended in a cave with both daughters made pregnant by him (Genesis 19:33–38). The sons they brought into the world were Moab and Ammon (Ben-ammi)—fathers to the Moabites and the Ammonites who are enemies of God's children, the Israelites, to this day. There are always results of our decisions.

Some of us are in a cave of our own making—carved out of a lifetime of decisions to do things our own way. Some see only with the "I" and not the "eye" of faith. Some have become hard and rigid as the pillar of salt because we insist on looking back —at some failure that still defeats us, or at some success that has become a stumbling block of pride.

Men of God   There are many other examples of faith—those who have left us a pattern of trust in Christ to follow.

Moses believed God against all the power of Pharaoh, and the children of Israel were taken from bondage and slavery in Egypt to the freedom of God in the Promised Land.

Joshua believed God, and the walls of Jericho fell—a military victory performed in a miraculous way.

Many stood for God and believed God against all odds. These He remembers in Hebrews 11—the beautiful Hall of Faith.

> For whatever is born of God overcomes the world; and this is the victory that has overcome the world—our faith.
>
> 1 John 5:4

> Trust in the Lord with all your heart,
> And do not lean on your own understanding.
> In all your ways acknowledge Him,
> And He will make your paths straight.
>
> Proverbs 3:5, 6

Let the Holy Spirit underline the word *all* on your heart and you will find your paths being directed by Him. You will see and pray with the eye of faith.

6

Warfare

It was midnight. The night was dark and the village was quiet as we walked down the empty street. Cal and I were in Huémoz, Switzerland, visiting the Schaeffers' community of ministry at L'Abri. We rented a room in one of the village chalets, and were walking toward that room. We had just finished a beautiful evening of fellowship. We had attended the meeting at the chapel, then we had tea with some dear people from Britain. It had been a beautiful week—L'Abri Festival of Arts. Our hearts had been very blessed as we witnessed God working in the lives of the young people.

We reached our chalet and the door was locked! We knocked gently, but there was no answer. We discovered later that another lodger had come in after the meeting and thought we were in. He had locked the door. God was in that decision!

Spiritual Battle   As we stood there, wondering what we were to do, we heard sobbing. It became louder and we started toward the sound. As we got nearer, we could see a young man bending over a sobbing girl lying prone on the street. Just as we got to them, there was a blood-curdling scream, and we could see that he was holding her down.

We recognized the man as a British actor we knew. As he realized who we were, he quickly said to Cal, "Please pray for her." Cal and I knelt down by our friend and we put our hands on the girl to help hold her. As we touched her, she screamed again. Cal began to pray for her and immediately he pleaded

the Blood of Jesus over her and us "in Jesus' Name." As he
pleaded the Blood, she kicked viciously and Cal carried the
mark on his leg for a long time. We knew from her violent
reaction to the Blood of Jesus and His Name—Jesus—as well as
other manifestations, that we were in the midst of satanic warfare.

As we continued to pray, she became increasingly loud.
Other young people gathered around, and about eight were
soon holding her down. Suddenly she pushed them all off and
ran a block down the village street and out into an open field.
She threw herself down and a number following knelt beside
her to continue prayer and ministry.

Our British friend asked us to go into one of the chalets with
him for prayer. A number of us gathered and prayed, beseech-
ing God for the deliverance of this dear girl. In a short time they
led her in. She came very quietly and was ministered to by the
group.

I trust she has been delivered! It was our first time to really
witness the warfare between Christ and Satan. The reality of
the battle shocked us. Other things about the battle had been
real. We had seen his vicious attacks on people, but had not seen
firsthand his control of an individual.

A Fallen Prince   Satan does have power to control. He has
his own kingdom. He is the "prince of the power of the air"
(Ephesians 2:2). In Isaiah 14 we read of his fall from heaven. He,
Lucifer, was beautiful and was lifted up in pride. God had to put
out of heaven both Satan and all the angels who were following
him. They are Satan's demons, those who do his bidding.

His kingdom is especially graphically described in the Living
Bible: "For we are not fighting against people made of flesh and
blood, but against persons without bodies—the evil rulers of the
unseen world, those mighty satanic beings and great evil
princes of darkness who rule this world; and against huge numbers of wicked spirits in the spirit world" (Ephesians 6:12 LB).

We know now that there are many who have given their lives

to Satan. Within the last few years, Satan worship has become very open, especially in San Francisco, California, where the headquarters of the satanic church is located.

The followers really do give their souls to Satan. They ask him to come in and they delight in his presence. They have to obey in only one important area. Each of them must love Satan with all his heart, soul, mind, and spirit. They must memorize Scripture backwards! The most powerful Scripture in reverse is the Lord's Prayer. The second most powerful is the Twenty-third Psalm. They break the cross of Jesus and also wear the cross upside down. They believe that they will be rewarded for the amount of evil they have done—when they get to hell. Murder, all kinds of sex perversion, and all types of sin are entered into with excitement and fiendish joy because it makes Satan happy. They have freedom for all things, not knowing that freedom for "things" is the strongest bondage possible. Satan is a hard taskmaster. The only true freedom is freedom in Christ.

They have their church services—their mass and communion in their own devilish ways. It is a complete mockery of Jesus and His Kingdom. I'm so grateful that Satan is a defeated foe and that we don't have to conquer him daily. *He was defeated at the cross.*

He sometimes appears as a roaring lion:

> Be careful—watch out for attacks from Satan, your great enemy. He prowls around like a hungry, roaring lion, looking for some victim to tear apart. Stand firm when he attacks. Trust the Lord; and remember that other Christians all around the world are going through these sufferings too.
>
> 1 Peter 5:8, 9 LB

He will devour those not in Christ. He does have control of their lives. They may seemingly prosper for a time, but God's judgment will eventually fall upon them.

Satan's Deceptions   He also can change his appearance into
an angel of light—someone beautiful and very alluring:

> God never sent those men at all; they are "phonies" who
> have fooled you into thinking they are Christ's apostles.
> Yet I am not surprised! Satan can change himself into an
> angel of light, so it is no wonder his servants can do it too,
> and seem like godly ministers. In the end they will get
> every bit of punishment their wicked deeds deserve.
>
> 2 Corinthians 11:13–15 LB

Satan knows that many of us as Christians hear his growl and are
on to his tricks. He has to find a different way to deceive us. He
appears as something beautiful—something good. For instance,
we may be tempted to neglect our Bible reading, our prayer,
and our fellowship with Christ—in order to do service for him.

We may be tested by finding ourselves resenting other Christian workers or being envious of them. We may find a church
riddled by the strife of tongues—people finding fault with one
another. These are people who would not think of murdering
another. This is an obvious temptation. But Satan uses the subtle
testings, gets a foothold, and hangs on. The advice of Scripture
is: "Do not give the devil an opportunity" (*see* Ephesians 4:27).

> Not every one that saith unto me, Lord, Lord, shall enter
> into the kingdom of heaven; but he that doeth the will
> of my Father which is in heaven. Many will say to me in
> that day, Lord, Lord, have we not prophesied in thy
> name? and in thy name have cast out devils? and in thy
> name done many wonderful works? And then will I pro-
> fess unto them, I never knew you: depart from me, ye
> that work iniquity.
>
> Matthew 7:21–23 KJV

This passage shows us that there are those unbelievers under Satan's control who will deceive the believers. When they appear before Jesus in that day, they will say, "Lord, Lord, have we not prophesied in thy name? and in thy name have cast out devils? and in thy name done many wonderful works?" Jesus will answer, "And then will I profess unto them, I never knew you: depart from me, ye that work iniquity."

Second Timothy tells of many "having a form of godliness, but denying the power thereof" (*see* 3:5 KJV). You notice it says *a form of godliness.* In this case, and in Matthew 7:21–23, we find unbelievers playing the roles of Christians, but lacking a life of Christ within.

The second time I saw Satan at work was in the life of a teenage girl. She had deliberately worshiped other gods, and was now seeking the true God. Satan was determined to keep her in his control. As we dealt with the demons within her, we discovered a number controlling her body. To name a few, there were demons of lust, fear, death, and pain. We had to believe that Jesus had defeated Satan, before this girl could be delivered. Before help can come, his defeat must be a reality to the people praying for deliverance. She had to renounce all of Satan's power over the different areas of her life in which she had bargained with him. Satan tried to keep her from coming to Christ. As she received Him, the death demon said he would kill her. She suffered excruciating pain, and he also tried to choke her. With the authority we have in Christ, we renounced Satan and he had to let go of her. He cannot keep a person from coming to Christ.

We worked with her for several days. She stayed with some Christian girls at night, and they surrounded her with God's love and care. God delivered her—but what warfare! When a life has been given to Satan, he wants to keep his control of that body. He gives up only after a real struggle. That person must then place full trust in Christ's keeping him, for Satan wants to reenter that body.

Satan bargains with people. He will promise fame, honor, new pleasure in sex, speaking ability, wealth, and other things —if we will give our lives to him. Demons do enter the body, in a mimicry of the Holy Spirit entering the life of one who has given himself to Christ. Sometimes Christians try to bargain with Satan. They tell him that they will leave him alone, if he will leave *them* alone. They naively believe that if they keep their part, he will keep his. He has them blinded and lulled to sleep.

Possession and Invasion   We feel that a believer in Christ cannot be possessed—that is, completely taken over. Only an unsaved one can be possessed. As believers, our spirits are one with Christ's; we are sealed in Him and nothing can change or touch this position. We believe with Dr. Merrill Unger that a Christian can be invaded. Dr. Unger states in *Demons in The World Today*, "It is possible for a believer to experience severe demon influence or obsession if he persistently yields to demonic temptation and sin." The mind, the part of us which will know each other in heaven, is in the soul. The mind can be invaded. A trip on drugs can open the mind to the entrance of demons. That mind was not under its owner's control when he or she was "spaced out" on drugs.

Some people become drunk and do not remember things that happened on a certain weekend or night. Their minds were not under their own control. At these times Satan can invade, and then he will sometimes control that person.

There are also other cases where a person who has been active in witchcraft, the occult, or the spirit world in some other way has come to Christ. There was cleansing from sin, but some have needed deliverance from demons after that.

The girl we just discussed had to have deliverance *after* salvation. The demons could not keep her from receiving Christ Jesus as her Saviour. After salvation, the Holy Spirit was within her, and the inner man was strengthened to defeat the demons.

She wanted help. <u>A person with demons cannot be helped</u> <u>unless he or she wants help</u>.

Signs of Demonic Activity   Some of the manifestations of demonic activity are:

1. A change of the eyes and face. The eyes may take on a wild look. The face can become hard and evil-looking.

2. Superhuman strength.

3. The person saying things he doesn't mean to say, such as swearing. Often he will either not know that he said it, or report that someone within him spoke.

4. A drastic change in behavior. This is not necessarily satanic activity. I cannot overemphasize this. Some illness can cause this change.

5. Deep depression. One also needs to be very careful about this. When a woman comes to me deeply depressed, I usually advise her to see her doctor for a checkup. We need Holy Spirit discernment to know where there is satanic activity. <u>There can</u> <u>be physical depression of the mind, and there can be</u> satanic <u>oppression.</u> "You know of Jesus of Nazareth, how God anointed Him with the Holy Spirit and with power, and how He went about doing good, and healing all who were oppressed by the devil; for God was with Him" (Acts 10:38). Physical depression responds to medication. Spiritual oppression responds only to our authority in Christ.

6. Speaking with another voice. We have heard a man's voice speaking through a woman.

7. Illness with no organic basis. The pain can move to different parts of the body. We need to be very careful with this, so that we not diagnose someone's illness as satanic when it is a real illness of the body.

8. A person hearing voices in his mind. The demons can talk to the person they inhabit. We have read in the papers of people who have said that a voice told them to kill another. Their

action was controlled by that voice.

9. Suicidal tendencies. This also may not be demonic. However, there are demons of suicide. When they are asked what their duty is, they will reply that it is to make that person commit suicide.

10. Uncontrollable fears. There are normal fears such as our feeling when we see a child run for the street, or know that a child is hurt. Demonic fear controls a person and makes him incapable of performance in a certain area.

11. Uncontrollable temper leading to violence. Caution needs to be used here. We all need the freedom to express ourselves. For one to be denied the freedom of showing the emotion of indignation means we may be stifling all emotions, including the ability to express love. The dictionary defines indignation as "righteous anger at what one considers unfair, mean, or shameful." Christ had this feeling as He cleansed the temple. His reaction to the sellers and money changers in the temple brought about His action in chasing them out. This is the same reaction we feel when we see a child mistreated. This must always be action under control. Rage and fury speak of uncontrollable actions. Our actions are to be under God's control. When we train a child we are to train his emotions, not just submerge them. There are correct outlets for feeling.

12. Deep anxieties. Of course, anxiety need not be demonic, but we have heard demons confess their names as "anxiety."

Torment goes with all of these signs. Satan causes deep torment and feelings of failure. Jesus cleansed the maniac of Gadara (Luke 8:26–39). "[The man] was possessed with demons; and [he] had not put on any clothing for a long time, and was not living in a house, but in the tombs. . . . For it [the unclean spirit] had seized him many times; and he was bound with chains and shackles and kept under guard; and yet he would burst his fetters and be driven by the demon into the desert" (vv. 27, 29).

The condition and torment of a demon-possessed person is clearly pictured here. He could not keep clothing on, and he lived in the cemetery. His superhuman strength is mentioned, as well as the fact that he was driven by the demon. Uncontrollable actions! In response to Jesus' question about his name, the demons answered, "Legion," meaning thousands. Jesus commanded them to come out and they did. They went into the pigs and caused unusual behavior in them—demons can inhabit animals.

In verse 35 we find the same man cleansed and delivered, sitting at Jesus' feet. He was clothed, and was in his right mind.

Cases of Demon Activity   We have worked with a number of cases of exorcism. Alice was one of them. She came to us wanting prayer for her severe physical problems. As we prayed for her, we detected demon activity. She wanted help and we arranged to have a group of Christians pray with her.

She had been very lonely and had spent many hours playing with the Ouija board. After a long period of communicating with it, a man's voice began to speak to her. Thereafter, when she was lonely, she would talk to the Ouija board and her "friend" would talk to her.

After months of this he talked her into a "spiritist's wedding." At the arranged time, her spirit left her body and joined together with his spirit in a "marriage ceremony." This opened her body to him and he is now a demon within her. He brought another demon with him, and this demon torments her most of the time. She wants us to get rid of the cruel demon, but wants to keep the demon she married in spirit. This one is the demon of lust. These are very common, and in almost every case of demon possession we have found a demon of lust.

We could not help Alice. We prayed for her and also prayed for the cleansing of her house. She herself cannot be delivered until she really wants help.

Cal and I were called in on a case which a Christian surgeon had diagnosed as demon activity. The doctor has also had three years of training in psychiatry, and we respected his ability and honesty in knowing her real need.

The patient had been acting strangely, and her boyfriend called for help. As we witnessed to her about Jesus Christ, her face changed, her eyes became glazed, and her body stiffened. She hissed like a snake and then growled like a wolf. The look from her eyes was pure hatred. Suddenly she lunged at my husband and had to be restrained. We knew this was satanic warfare.

The call went out for the Christians who had been ministering together in exorcism. They gathered quickly and began reading their Bibles and praying. One of the ministers was dealing with Judy, the demon-possessed girl. At times we all read the same passage aloud. We sang hymns about the Blood. I especially remember the violent reaction she had as we read Psalm 23, which is about Jesus, and the demons' hatred of Him was very apparent as they caused Judy's body to thrash about wildly. She was alternately hissing and growling.

Judy did not know she was acting strangely. This was blocked from her conscious mind. As she noticed people gathering, she asked why people were there. Her friend told her that he had needed help with her, and we had come. She wanted to know why, so he explained her behavior to her and told her we felt it was satanic activity. She believed him and wanted help. Judy had been aware that at times she would "come to herself" in a room and not remember going there. It had also happened in her car. She had "come to herself" and found herself driving in a strange area, not knowing how she got there.

From the time she decided she wanted help, we had difficulty keeping her conscious. Satan would "zap" her—that is, she would just suddenly be unconscious. We would have to use our authority in Christ and command the demons to let go of her. As she was witnessed to about Jesus, she decided to receive Him as her Saviour. Immediately she was "zapped." Again and again, as she tried to voice the words *I love Jesus,* she went unconscious before she could say them.

Satan at one time took her hearing—she just became deaf. She was able to tell us. We prayed, rebuking Satan, and her hearing was restored. Then Satan took her voice. Her vocal cords were paralyzed. She had to point to her mouth and shake her head.

We got a pen and a paper plate for her. I think it was the first piece of paper we found. She took the pen in her hand and Satan paralyzed her arm. She held her writing hand steady with her other hand. There was much prayer and, although Satan gave much resistance by holding her hand away from the paper and by "zapping" her, she did write the words *I love Jesus.* There was much praise in the room and we were thankful that her voice returned with the victory.

We took turns working with Judy for several days. The demons had to come out. Now, with the Holy Spirit within, she had all of the authority and power of God. She joined us in commanding that they leave.

Judy's story was a sad one. When she was younger, a stranger had followed her at a distance for a long period of time, as she went to and from school. One day he kidnapped her and took her to a lonely spot on the desert. He used her nude body as an altar on which to worship Satan. He killed an animal and used parts of the animal's body on hers. This ceremony of lust and commitment to Satan went on for three days. Somehow she got away from him and to safety. Many things happened as a result of this episode, and she has had difficulties ever since.

One of the strangest happenings was in the hospital as she was recovering from surgery. A woman in another bed in the room had had the same type of surgery. One morning Judy woke at four to find the other woman mumbling strange words over her. She asked her what she was doing and she replied, "I have work to do." Judy noticed that she walked with no crutch or help of any kind, even though her leg was in a cast. This same thing happened three mornings in a row.

The woman was from England, and Judy found out that she was a witch. She had been sent over here to do certain work. She had had surgery once before on her leg, but had not taken care of it because she wanted to go back into the hospital to finish her "work."

The Holy Spirit sends us to other Christians in need—and others to us in our need. Even so, in the Satan kingdom, they are sent to do Satan's bidding. He is their master.

We did see deliverance for this precious girl. There were many demons there, but they had to go—and they did. They have no power when Jesus Christ's power is appropriated. The warfare really is between Jesus and Satan. We are hidden in Christ. When we neglect to abide, we are out there in the open arena doing battle by ourselves. We will be defeated. Christ defeated Satan at the cross, but he is still a powerful enemy here.

An Example From Daniel   We read an unusual story:

In the third year of the reign of Cyrus, king of Persia, Daniel (also called Belteshazzar) had another vision. It concerned events certain to happen in the future: times of great tribulation—wars and sorrows, and this time he understood what the vision meant.

When this vision came to me (Daniel said later) I had been in mourning for three full weeks. All that time I tasted neither wine nor meat, and of course I went without desserts. I neither washed nor shaved nor combed my hair.

Then one day early in April, as I was standing beside the great Tigris River, I looked up and suddenly there before me stood a person robed in linen garments, with a belt of purest gold around his waist, and glowing, lustrous skin! From his face came blinding flashes like lightning, and his eyes were pools of fire; his arms and feet shown like polished brass, and his voice was like the roaring of a vast multitude of people.

I, Daniel, alone saw this great vision; the men with me saw nothing, but they were suddenly filled with unreasoning terror and ran to hide, and I was left alone. When I saw this frightening vision my strength left me, and I grew pale and weak with fright.

Then he spoke to me, and I fell to the ground face downward in a deep faint. But a hand touched me and lifted me, still trembling, to my hands and knees. And I heard his voice—"O Daniel, greatly beloved of God," he said, "stand up and listen carefully to what I have to say to you, for God has sent me to you." So I stood up, still trembling with fear.

Then he said, "Don't be frightened, Daniel, for your request has been heard in heaven and was answered the very first day you began to fast before the Lord and pray for understanding; that very day I was sent here to meet you. But for twenty-one days the mighty Evil Spirit who overrules the kingdom of Persia blocked my way. Then Michael, one of the top officers of the heavenly army, came to help me, so that I was able to break through these spirit rulers of Persia."

Daniel 10:1–13 LB

Daniel prayed and fasted (a partial fast) for twenty-one days. At the end of that time, a heavenly being came to him with the answer, but told him that God started him on the way with his answer the first day he, Daniel, prayed. A mighty evil prince of

Persia (*see* Ephesians 6:12) was able to block his way for the twenty-one-day period. God sent Michael, one of His chief princes, to help Him get the answer to Daniel.

Now I began to understand Luke 18:1 ". . . men ought always to pray, and not to lose heart—not to faint" (*see* KJV).

Satan has power to detain our prayers. Keep praying! When you pray, believe! God loves to answer. "This poor man cried and the Lord heard him; And saved him out of all his troubles" (Psalms 34:6).

The Power of Faith   Remember that you pray with His faith (Galatians 2:20; 5:22, 23). In Romans 12:3 every believer is given a measure of faith. How big a measure do *you* hold up to Him? Jesus said, "According to your faith be it [done] unto you" (Matthew 9:29 KJV) and, "Have faith in God. Truly I say to you, whoever says to this mountain, 'Be taken up and cast into the sea,' and does not doubt in his heart, but believes that what he says is going to happen, it shall be granted him" (Mark 11:22, 23).

Christ promises His disciples power for service as they wait on Him: "But you shall receive power when the Holy Spirit has come upon you; and you shall be My witnesses both in Jerusalem, and in all Judea and Samaria, and even to the remotest part of the earth" (Acts 1:8). We are also told in Colossians 1:11 that we are "strengthened with all power" for this battle "according to His glorious might."

Paul prays that we might ". . . know the love of Christ which surpasses knowledge, that you may be filled up to all the fulness of God. Now to Him who is able to do exceeding abundantly beyond all that we ask or think [or even dream of], according to the power that works within us, to Him be the glory in the church and in Christ Jesus to all generations forever and ever. Amen" (Ephesians 3:19–21). *Ye shall receive power—strengthened with all power according to the power that works within us.* He will do exceeding abundantly above all we ask, think, or dream of. What power? The same power that raised our Christ Jesus from the dead.

"That your faith should not rest on the wisdom of men, but on the power of God" (1 Corinthians 2:5). This is His power which is God in us. We have all the power of God flowing through us. In Ephesians 5:18 we are told to be filled with the Spirit. He comes in as we are born again. When we are emptied of self, we give Him these areas of our lives. The Holy Spirit fills this new place.

Let bitterness go—let envy and strife go—let jealousies and angers go! Let anything go that would keep the power of God from flowing through you. As we are cleansed of sin, of negative attitudes and wrong actions, God's love can flow through us. "The love of God is shed abroad in our hearts by the Holy Spirit" (*see* Romans 5:5 KJV). God pours His love through. Many of us are like the Dead Sea. The power and love of God are there, but our negative attitudes hinder the flow outward, causing us to become stagnant.

Satan knows where our weak areas are, and we are no match for him by ourselves. In our work with people who have demons, we have found the demon watching the Christians in the room. I've heard a demon point out a weakness or a sin in one of their lives. We have to examine and keep examining ourselves in this battle to be sure we keep ourselves cleansed and abiding in Him. Where there is sin in a life, Christ's power cannot flow to the healing and cleansing of others.

It is of the utmost importance that we believe God has given us His power and authority for this battle. As you know warfare and are alert to Satan's tactics, you can use your authority in Christ. Then you can trust to be in the place of victory daily.

In the following chapters we discuss Christ's armor of protection for us and the weapons He gives us to use.

Psalm 121 is a great comfort to me as I think of this warfare:

Shall I look to the mountain gods for help? No! My help is from Jehovah who made the mountains! And the heavens too! He will never let me stumble, slip or fall. For he is always watching, never sleeping.

Jehovah himself is caring for you! He is your defender. He protects you day and night. He keeps you from all evil, and preserves your life. He keeps his eye upon you as you come and go, and always guards you.

Psalms 121:1–8 LB

7

Armor

The spiritual warfare is described for us in Ephesians 6:12. God has promised us all we may need at any time and He has given the armor for this warfare: "The night is almost gone, and the day is at hand. Let us therefore lay aside the deeds of darkness and put on the armor of light" (Romans 13:12). Jesus said, "I am the light of the world; he who follows Me shall not walk in the darkness, but shall have the light of life" (John 8:12).

The Armor of Light   Christ is the Light of the World. As we put on the armor of light, we are actually putting on Christ Himself. It is the picture of abiding in Him (*see* John 15). We fight the spiritual warfare from this position.

Christ tells us that *we* are the light of the world. As we are hidden in Jesus, His light shines through us. The world is a brighter place because God has placed Christians everywhere. "Let your light shine before men in such a way that they may see your good works, and glorify your Father who is in heaven" (Matthew 5:16).

Satan knows where God's lights are. He is very much aware that the power which generates the Christian's light is much greater than his (Satan's) power. As the light is cleansed and the power flows out, Christ's battles are won.

"Finally, be strong in the Lord, and in the strength of His might. Put on the full armor of God, that you may be able to

stand firm against the schemes of the devil" (Ephesians 6:10, 11).
The Living Bible calls them "strategies and tricks of Satan." We
are alerted to the fact that there is a warfare—that Satan has a
very real, unseen kingdom (Ephesians 6:12 LB). In order to
stand, we must obey Christ and put on the armor He tells us to.

When we were sending men to Vietnam for war, many were
taken to a village in the United States, such as they would find
in Vietnam, and outfitted with the armor they would need
there. They were also given weapons appropriate for that particular warfare and trained in their use.

How much more will God do that for us, His beloved children! He does not want us defeated in this battle and He has
provided the way for our deliverance. The armor is named for
us in Ephesians 6:13–18, and we have been told: "Put on the
full armor of God [all of it], that you may be able to stand firm
against the schemes of the devil" (v. 11, *italics* added).

Satan's kingdom, with its ranks and personalities, is described: "For our struggle is not against flesh and blood, but
. . . against the spiritual forces of wickedness in the heavenly
places. Therefore, take up the full armor of God, that you may
be able to resist in the evil day, and having done everything, to
stand firm" (vv. 12, 13).

The Girdle of Truth and Righteousness   "Stand firm therefore, having girded your loins with truth, and having put on the
breastplate of righteousness" (Ephesians 6:14).

The *girdle* was the piece of clothing which held the garment
together and kept it on. The girdle of truth—the piece that
covers the lower part of the body—is Christ Himself. He said,
"I am the way, the truth, and the life: no man cometh unto the
Father, but by me" (John 14:6 KJV). He also referred to His
Father as being Truth, in John 7:28 and John 8:26.

The *breastplate* covering the chest is righteousness and this
also is Christ. "Christ Jesus became to us righteousness" (*see* 1
Corinthians 1:30). His righteousness becomes ours. God sees us

not in our old sins, but in the righteousness of Christ Jesus, my Lord.

The Shoes of Peace   Ephesians 6:15 tells us of the armor for our *feet.* They are to be shod "with the preparation of the gospel of peace." Also: "And how shall they preach unless they are sent? Just as it is written, 'How beautiful are the feet of those who bring glad tidings of good things!' " (Romans 10:15). The Living Bible reads: "And how will anyone go and tell them unless someone sends him? That is what the Scriptures are talking about when they say, 'How beautiful are the feet of those who . . . bring glad tidings of good things. . . .' "

In the Old Testament:

> How lovely on the mountains
> Are the feet of him who brings good news,
> Who announces peace
> And brings good news of happiness,
> Who announces salvation,
> And says to Zion, "Your God reigns!"
>
> Isaiah 52:7

The Living Bible reads: "How beautiful upon the mountains are the feet of those who bring the happy news of peace and salvation, the news that the God of Israel reigns."

The shoes of our armor are peace.

> For He Himself is our peace, who made both groups into one, and broke down the barrier of the dividing wall, by abolishing in His flesh the enmity, which is the Law of commandments contained in ordinances, that in Himself He might make the two into one new man, thus establishing peace, and might reconcile them both in one body to God through the cross, by it having put to death the enmity. And He came and preached peace to you

who were far away, and peace to those who were near; for through Him we both have our access in one Spirit to the Father.

Ephesians 2:14–18

He, Christ, is our peace. Our feet also are to be hidden *in* Him, to be covered *by* Him. "As you therefore have received Christ Jesus the Lord, so walk in Him" (Colossians 2:6). We are to wear shoes that speed us on. Jesus sends us out to be His witnesses and He, our peace, is our message.

The Shield of Faith   "In addition to all, taking up the *shield of faith* with which you will be able to extinguish all the flaming missiles of the evil one" (Ephesians 6:16, *italics* added). The Living Bible reads: "In every battle you will need faith as your shield to stop the fiery arrows aimed at you by Satan." King James speaks of "fiery darts."

The shield is the piece which can be moved to cover any part of the body at which Satan is shooting. The shield is faith. We have discussed at length the importance of our faith and trust in Him. It is so necessary that we trust Him to keep us. We cannot keep ourselves. We go down in defeat.

This poor man cried and the Lord heard him;
And saved him out of all his troubles.

Psalms 34:6

The Lord will protect you from all evil;
He will keep your soul.

Psalms 121:7

Shall I look to the mountain gods for help? No! My help is from Jehovah who made the mountains! And the heav-

mind of Christ. ". . . . But we have the mind of Christ" (1 Corinthians 2:16). One of His riches I appropriate is His mind. He is the covering for my head in this battle for the control of my mind and body.

The Sword of His Word   The last part of Ephesians 6:17 reads: ". . . and the *sword of the Spirit,* which is the *word* of God" (*italics* added). We are to take the sword. "For the word of God is living and active and sharper than any two-edged sword, and piercing as far as the division of soul and spirit, of both joints and marrow, and able to judge the thoughts and intentions of the heart" (Hebrews 4:12).

The Word—the Bible—is the sword for this battle. It is alive, it is active and it is sharper than any two-edged sword. A two-edged sword cuts any way you use it. So does the Word. It is sharp.

A note of caution is needed here. Because the Word does cut, we must be very careful to use it under the guidance of the Holy Spirit. If we quote it in the flesh, trying to defend a point or trying to show someone his sin, we can cut another very badly. He is just cut and hurt. Where we use the Word under the direction of the Holy Spirit, hearts are blessed. The revealing and the cutting away of sin is accomplished, but it is done by Him. People are blessed and lives are changed. Where the Holy Spirit is doing the cutting through the Word, He uses His own anesthetic—the love of God which sustains us in all our testings.

The Word of God is cleansing. "That He might sanctify her [the church, His bride], having cleansed her by the washing of water with the word" (Ephesians 5:26). In John: "You are already clean because of the word which I have spoken to you" (15:3). As we use the sword which is the Word, in this battle, we will see great victories for God. I will further discuss this weapon, this part of the armor, as I discuss the weapons of warfare.

We are to take the *sword* of the Spirit, which is the Word of

God. In this picture we are to put on the armor, take our position in Him and: "With all prayer and petition pray at all times
in the Spirit, and with this in view, be on the alert with all
perseverance and petition for all the saints" (Ephesians 6:18).
The Living Bible reads, "Pray all the time. Ask God for anything
in line with the Holy Spirit's wishes. Plead with him, reminding
him of your needs, and keep praying earnestly for all Christians
everywhere."

Full Armor   What an encouraging picture—as we face the
battle with Satan. Christ Himself is my complete armor.

The girdle of truth is Christ Himself. He is holding it all
together.

The breastplate of righteousness is His righteousness and
becomes mine at the cross. Satan cannot defeat me with the sins
I have confessed. I am clothed in His righteousness.

My shoes are His peace. I walk in peace.

My shield of protection against fiery arrows or darts is His
faith which He has also given to me. I must practice using the
shield. This battle requires skill.

My head is covered with Him who is my *helmet of salvation.*
His salvation is healing, cleansing, and saving. His salvation is
mine.

The sword placed in my hand is His Word. This also takes
practice. It must be taken up and used to be effective. So must
we take up the Word of God to be effective participants in this
battle.

Last, but not least, the battle is not ours, but the Lord's.
". . . Do not fear or be dismayed because of this great multitude,
for the battle is not yours but God's" (2 Chronicles 20:15). As we
stand, dressed in this armor He has given, He fights the battle
for us! We learn that the victory is "not by might nor by power,
but by My Spirit, says the Lord of hosts" (*see* Zechariah 4:6).

8

The Weapons for Warfare

God has given us weapons for this warfare. Jesus always meets us at our point of need, and when we battle with Satan, it must be with Christ's weapons. "Put on the full armor of God, that you may be able to stand firm against the schemes of the devil" (Ephesians 6:11). The Living Bible reads: "Put on all of God's armor so that you will be able to stand safe against all strategies and tricks of Satan."

For though we walk in the flesh, we do not war according to the flesh, for the weapons of our warfare are not of the flesh, but divinely powerful for the destruction of fortresses. We are destroying speculations and every lofty thing raised up against the knowledge of God, and we are taking every thought captive to the obedience of Christ, and we are ready to punish all disobedience, whenever your obedience is complete.

2 Corinthians 10:3–6

It is true that I am an ordinary, weak human being, but I don't use human plans and methods to win my battles. I use God's mighty weapons, not those made by men, to knock down the devil's strongholds. These weapons can break down every proud argument against God and every wall that can be built to keep men from finding him.

With these weapons I can capture rebels and bring them back to God, and change them into men whose hearts' desire is obedience to Christ. I will use these weapons against every rebel who remains after I have first used them on you yourselves, and you surrender to Christ.

                              2 Corinthians 10:3–6 LB

Thou art my King, O God;
Command victories for Jacob.
Through Thee we will push back our adversaries;
Through Thy name we will trample down those
        who rise up against us.
For I will not trust in my bow,
Nor will my sword save me.
But Thou hast saved us from our adversaries,
And Thou hast put to shame those who hate us.
In God we have boasted all day long,
And we will give thanks to Thy name forever.

                                   Psalms 44:4–8

You are my King and my God. Decree victories for your people. For it is only by your power and through your name that we tread down our enemies. I do not trust my weapons. They could never save me. Only you can give us victory over those who hate us. My constant boast is God. I can never thank you enough!

                                Psalms 44:4–8 LB

Paul says we are not to receive the grace of God in vain; we are to give no cause for offense:

But in everything commending ourselves as servants of God, in much endurance, in afflictions, in hardships, in distresses, in beatings, in imprisonments, in tumults, in labors, [in watchings, in fastings], in purity, in knowledge, in patience, in kindness, in the Holy Spirit, in genuine love, in the word of truth, in the power of God; by the weapons of righteousness for the right hand and the left, by glory and dishonor, by evil report and good report; regarded as deceivers and yet true; as unknown yet well-known, as dying yet behold, we live; as punished yet not put to death, as sorrowful yet always rejoicing, as poor yet making many rich, as having nothing yet possessing all things.

2 Corinthians 6:4–10

Notice verse 7: ". . . by the weapons of righteousness for the right hand and the left." The Living Bible reads: "We have been truthful with God's power helping us in all we do. All of the godly man's arsenals—weapons of defense, and weapons of attack—have been ours."

In 1 Timothy 1:18 Paul encourages Timothy, his spiritual son, to "fight the good fight." The King James Version reads: "That thou by them mightest war a good warfare." The Living Bible has been paraphrased to read: "Fight well in the Lord's battles. . . ."

Spiritual Weapons   It is clear from these Scriptures that there are weapons for our battle with Satan. We have just discussed the armor and now we will talk about the weapons. They are not something we can take hold of and use as we would a gun. Because the battle is in the heavenlies (Ephesians 6:12), we must use spiritual warfare.

[Jesus says:] "Do you not believe that I am in the Father, and the Father is in Me? The words that I say to you I do not speak on My own initiative, but the Father abiding in Me does His works. Believe Me and I am in the Father,

and the Father in Me; otherwise believe on account of
the works themselves. Truly, truly, I say to you, he who
believes in Me, the works that I do shall he do also; and
greater works than these shall he do; because I go to the
Father."

John 14:10–12

In verse 10 He explains that He is in the Father and the
Father in Him. He speaks what the Father tells Him to and the
His Life Father abiding in Him does the works.

In verse 11 He asks them to believe that He is in the Father
and the Father is in Him, or else believe because of the works
themselves.

In verse 12 He tells us that if we believe Him we will do the
His promise works that He does, and even greater works because He goes
to the Father.

In verses 13 and 14 we are given a prayer promise to go
with this startling verse. We are told to ask and He will do it.
our response In verse 15 He says, "If you love Me, you will keep My commandments." Our prayer answer hinges on this relationship. If
we do not believe that the Father was doing the works through
Him, we doubt His Word and do not love Him. There is no
prayer communication there.

While Jesus was here, the Father did the works through Him.
What works? What did Jesus do? He healed the blind, He made
the deaf hear and the lame walk. He fed the multitudes,
changed the weather and performed so many other miracles.
Remember—the Father was doing this through Him:

Jesus therefore answered and was saying to them,
"Truly, truly, I say to you, the Son can do nothing of
Himself, unless it is something He sees the Father do-
ing; for whatever the Father does, these things the
Son also does in like manner. For the Father loves the

Son, and shows Him all things that He Himself is doing; and greater works than these will He show Him,
that you may marvel. For just as the Father raises the
dead and gives them life, even so the Son also gives
life to whom He wishes."

John 5:19–21

He says that if we believe, we will do these works also, and
greater ones because He was going to the Father (John 14:12).
The Holy Spirit will do them through us, even as the Father did
them through the Son. It is not that we have reached some great
plateau of prayer; it is the power of God moving through us.
The greater works will be done as Christians everywhere believe and trust God for works to be done through them. In His
human nature, Jesus was limited to one place. With believers
around the world we can believe with Him for the greater
works that will be done.

Our weapons, then, are used in prayer and in the context of
John 14:10–15. This is closet prayer and should not be prayed
openly unless all understand. As we search the Scriptures, we
find three main weapons which are talked about.

The Blood of the Lamb   The first one we want to discuss is
the Blood shed on the cross. In Exodus 12 we read the story of
the Passover, first celebrated in Egypt. The children of Israel
had come down to Egypt in Joseph's time because of the fam-
ine. They had become a large nation, and the Egyptians had
made slaves of them to keep them from becoming too strong
and aggressive.

God raised up Moses to lead them out of Egypt into the
Promised Land. There had been much dickering with Pharaoh,
but nothing had been accomplished. They had already been
through nine plagues. There was to be one last plague. Then
Pharaoh would release the children of Israel. There was to be

a death in every home. In each household the firstborn child
and the firstborn cattle would die. The sin had to be punished
by death, but God told the children of Israel that the death in
their homes did not need to be one of their family. They could
have a substitute—a spotless lamb. What a beautiful picture!
John says, ". . . Behold, the Lamb of God who takes away the
sin of the world!" (John 1:29). He, God's firstborn, died as my
substitute.

They were told to take the spotless lamb and to kill it, catch-
ing the blood in a basin. They were to take a bunch of hyssop,
dip it into the blood, and strike the top and both sides of the
door. Actually, they were making the sign of the cross. They
were to be sure that their family was all in their house—with
the blood applied for protection. This was the place of safety.
God said: "When I see the blood, I will pass over you" (*see*
Exodus 12:13). God always provides a place of safety for His own
—He is our hiding place.

God kept His word. As they obeyed His commandment, the
death angel did pass over each house. "And they overcame him
because of the blood of the Lamb and because of the word of
their testimony, and they did not love their life even to death"
(Revelation 12:11). They overcame him (Satan—in this context)
by the Blood of the Lamb. The Blood shed by Christ on the cross
defeated Satan and he is forever defeated. He hates the Blood.
"And through Him to reconcile all things to Himself, having
made peace through the blood of His cross; through Him, I say,
whether things on earth or things in heaven" (Colossians 1:20).
He reconciled everything in heaven and earth to Himself, by
the Blood of His cross.

The Name of Jesus   The second weapon is the Name of
Jesus.

> Therefore also God highly exalted Him, and bestowed on
> Him the name which is above every name, that at the

name of Jesus every knee should bow, of those who are in heaven, and on earth, and under the earth, and that every tongue should confess that Jesus Christ is Lord, to the glory of God the Father.

Philippians 2:9–11

We are told that at the Name of Jesus every knee shall bow. In Acts 3:6 we read: "But Peter said, 'I do not possess silver and gold, but what I do have I give to you: In the name of Jesus Christ the Nazarene—walk!' "

And when they had placed them in the center, they began to inquire, "By what power, or in what name, have you done this?" Then Peter, filled with the Holy Spirit, said to them, "Rulers and elders of the people, if we are on trial today for a benefit done to a sick man, as to how this man has been made well, let it be known to all of you, and to all the people of Israel, that by the name of Jesus Christ the Nazarene, whom you crucified, whom God raised from the dead—by this name this man stands here before you in good health. He is the stone which was rejected by you, the builders, but which became the very corner stone. And there is salvation in no one else; for there is no other name under heaven that has been given among men, by which we must be saved."

Acts 4:7–12

Miracles were performed in the Name of Jesus Christ the Nazarene. Jesus said to pray in His Name (John 14:13). There is tremendous power in that Name, even as in the Blood shed on the cross. ". . . thou shalt call his name JESUS: for he shall save his people from their sins" (Matthew 1:21 KJV). The Name reminds Satan who it was that defeated him.

The Word of God   The third weapon is the Word of God, the Bible.

> For the word of God is living and active and sharper than any two-edged sword, and piercing as far as the division of soul and spirit, of both joints and marrow, and able to judge the thoughts and intentions of the heart.
>
>   Hebrews 4:12

The Word is a sword, and sharper than any two-edged sword. It does cut. In fact, it cuts through Satan's power. Christ Himself quoted the Word three times as Satan tempted Him (Matthew 4:1–11).

Satan hates the Blood shed on the cross. He hates the cross as much as the Blood. His intense hatred carries through to the Name of Jesus and on to the Word. Satan's goal is to keep people from coming to Christ. He cannot! When someone does come, he tries to keep him from having any rewards. He tries to make him as miserable a Christian as possible. Satan wants to keep us from knowing that he was defeated and that we really do have power and authority over him.

The Gift of Authority   It is important not only to know the weapons, but also to know our position in Christ. We must believe that we have the authority to use these weapons. This position is available to a child of God and the authority given to us is a result of our relationship with Him.

"Blessed be the God and Father of our Lord Jesus Christ, who has blessed us with every spiritual blessing in the heavenly places in Christ" (Ephesians 1:3). We are told that the Lord Jesus Christ *has blessed us with every spiritual blessing in the heavenly places in Christ.* The battle with Satan is in the lower heavens. Ephesians also tells us that in Christ we are far above all of Satan's kingdoms (6:12). Jesus told the high priest at His trial that He would be sitting at the right hand of power (Matthew 26:64). He is seated there now. "Who [Jesus] is at the right hand of God, having gone into heaven, after angels and authorities and powers had been subjected to Him" (1 Peter 3:22). We are told that: "[God] raised us up with Him, and seated us with Him in the heavenly places, in Christ Jesus" (Ephesians 2:6).

> Now you are no longer strangers to God and foreigners to heaven, but you are members of God's very own family, citizens of God's country, and you belong in God's household with every other Christian. What a foundation you stand on now: the apostles and the prophets; and the cornerstone of the building is Jesus Christ himself! We who believe are carefully joined together with Christ as parts of a beautiful, constantly growing temple for God. And you also are joined with him and with each other by the Spirit, and are part of this dwelling place of God.
>
> Ephesians 2:19–22 LB

How marvelous that we are no longer strangers and foreigners, but citizens—members of God's own family. The Holy Spirit has sealed us in this position. "In Him, you also, after listening to the message of truth, the gospel of your salvation—having also believed, you were sealed in Him with the Holy Spirit of promise" (Ephesians 1:13). You were sealed in Him. We are kept *by* Him. In John 17:11 Jesus asks the Father to keep us through His own Name.

We must believe that we are His children, born of God (John 1:12), and that He, as He promised, has given us all things in Christ. "So then let no one boast in men. For all things belong to you, whether Paul or Apollos or Cephas or the world or life or death or things present or things to come; all things belong to you, and you belong to Christ; and Christ belongs to God" (1 Corinthians 3:21–23).

From this position high above with Him, and having been given all things, let's examine the authority and power we have in Christ. We read in Ephesians: "In whom [Christ] we have boldness and confident access through faith in Him" (3:12). *We have boldness and access to Him.*

[Jesus said,] "Behold, I have given you authority to tread upon serpents and scorpions, and over all the power of the enemy. . . ."

Luke 10:19

And He called the twelve together, and gave them power and authority over all the demons, and to heal diseases.

Luke 9:1

[Christ said,] "All authority has been given to Me in heaven and on earth."

Matthew 28:18

Then He told them to go and make disciples of all the nations.

[And He said to them,] "You are witnesses of these things. And behold, I am sending forth the promise of My Father upon you; but you are to stay in the city until you are clothed with power from on high."

Luke 24:48, 49

He told His disciples to tarry until they were filled with the power of God. They were given a job to do, but were commanded to wait until God gave His power for service.

Divine Power   Let us refer back to John 14:12: ". . . the works that I do shall [you] do also; and greater works than these shall [you] do; because I go to the Father."

Remember, God did the work through Him. With what power? All of God's own mighty power. Paul prays that we may know ". . . what is the exceeding greatness of his power to us-ward who believe, according to the working of his mighty power, Which he wrought in Christ, when he raised him from the dead, and set him at his own right hand in the heavenly places, Far above all principality, and power, and might, and dominion, and every name that is named, not only in this world, but also in that which is to come: And hath put all things under his feet, and gave him to be the head over all things to the church, Which is his body, the fulness of him that filleth all in all" (Ephesians 1:19–23 KJV).

"And to know the love of Christ which surpasses knowledge, that you may be filled up to all the fulness of God. Now to Him who is able to do exceeding abundantly beyond all that we ask or think, according to the power that works within us" (Ephesians 3:19, 20).

Jesus taught with power and authority (Luke 4:32).

> [He said], All power is given unto me in heaven and in earth. Go ye therefore. . . .
>
> Matthew 28:18, 19 KJV

> He said to them, ". . . but you shall receive power when the Holy Spirit has come upon you; and you shall be My witnesses both in Jerusalem, and in all Judea and Samaria, and even to the remotest part of the earth."
>
> Acts 1:7, 8

> [Jesus said,] "Behold, I have given you authority to tread upon serpents and scorpions, and over all the power of the enemy, and nothing shall injure you."
>
> Luke 10:19

We, then, as believers appropriating God's gifts, receive this power and authority because He gives it to us. It is His will that we have power and not only have it—but use it.

Let me give you an illustration: Suppose you received a letter from someone very wealthy. The letter stated that this person had put a million dollars in your bank account. You found a bankbook enclosed with the letter. What would you do? Probably some would laugh, thinking it was a joke, and throw it all in the wastebasket. Someone else might call the bank and ask, "Did he really do this for me?" A third person might sit down and write a check.

Jesus said, *"Behold, I have given you authority . . . and you shall receive power."* He also said we would do these works the same as He. We, as we are in Christ, use the authority and power flowing through us for these works. Remember, we use His authority and power in prayer. The same thing is true spiritually. We have all of His riches, but must appropriate them.

Appropriating the Power   Some people feel too unworthy to accept this power. It is His worthiness that makes us righteous. If we look only at our unworthiness instead of Christ's worthiness, we are looking at ourselves, not Christ. This was Paul's problem in Romans 7. He used the pronoun *I* about thirty times. He was trying to shape up his old nature. In Romans 8:1 he had his eyes on Christ and said: "There is therefore now no condemnation for those who are in Christ Jesus."

The policeman who directs traffic at the corner is given the authority by the police department. It is delegated authority because he is serving them. He has been trained and given power by them to stop the cars, to tell them to move along, or anything that is needed to do the job his superiors give him to do. If I were to stand there and try to direct traffic it would only look foolish! He stands in his uniform, given him by the department. He raises his hand and traffic stops. It is not because of *who he is*. I don't need to know his name or a thing about him.

Traffic stops because of the authority and power given to him to carry out the orders of his supervisor.

This is a picture of us in prayer. We stand in Him, dressed in His righteousness and the full armor of God (Ephesians 6). We have in our hand the Word of God—the sword—to cut through Satan's power. Over the other arm we have the shield of faith to protect us from Satan's fiery darts. The Blood shed on the cross has been applied to us, and we battle in the Name of Jesus. We are ready to battle in prayer with this power and authority delegated to us.

We read: "Now may the God of peace Himself sanctify you entirely; and may your spirit and soul and body be preserved complete, without blame at the coming of our Lord Jesus Christ" (1 Thessalonians 5:23). God is Three—Father, Son, and Holy Spirit. We are made in His image. This verse says, "spirit and soul and body."

"For the word of God is living and active and sharper than any two-edged sword, and piercing as far as the division of soul and spirit, of both joints and marrow, and able to judge the thoughts and intentions of the heart" (Hebrews 4:12). *Soul* and *spirit* are listed separately here. The spirit is sealed in Christ (Ephesians 1:13). We are "one spirit with Him" (1 Corinthians 6:17). Nothing can touch this position in Him.

The mind is in the soul. The brain—the organ—is part of the body. The mind, the part of us that will know each other when we get to heaven, is in the soul.

The body is the display case for the spirit and soul and is the end result of the life spiritually. The body reveals our attitudes and priorities. It is imperfect and will be left here when the spirit and soul are released. We won't need this old body anymore. God has a new one for us (1 Corinthians 15:51; Philippians 3:21).

Pray for the Spirit   Paul says, "I pray for you spirit, soul and body." How would one pray for a *spirit?* Some requests are for the spirit, some are for the soul, and some are for the body.

To really have a fresh new love for God, day by day, is a spiritual blessing. It renews us in the inner (spirit) man. Only the Holy Spirit can give us this love. We can ask for it.

To really want to read the Word—and to know what we are reading—is a spiritual blessing. Many times I would rather take up something else to read. How relieved I was when my husband shared with me that he had a difficult time reading and praying. I thought I was the only one with that problem! Sometimes I have to ask Christ Jesus to pick up my Bible for me, and I try to remember to ask Him to teach me. What a difference it makes when He does the teaching.

To really love to pray is a spiritual blessing. We can read and not know a word we have read. We can go to a prayer meeting or even pray with others and not really know what was voiced in prayer. The Holy Spirit must read and pray through us for any lasting work to be accomplished.

To really look for Jesus' coming again, to really love other Christians, and to really love to go to God's House are all spiritual blessings. These things all affect the soul and body. We can ask for all of these blessings for ourselves and others.

Pray for the Soul   How would one pray for another's *soul?* We read, "Come to Me, all who are weary and heavy-laden, and I will give you rest. Take My yoke upon you, and learn from Me, for I am gentle and humble in heart; and you shall find rest for your souls. For My yoke is easy, and My load is light" (Matthew 11:28–30). God does give rest for the soul. What happens to the soul, and the mind which is in the soul, greatly affects the body. We can pray for soul-rest for people and for ourselves.

I urge you therefore, brethren, by the mercies of God, to present your bodies a living and holy sacrifice, acceptable to God, which is your spiritual service of worship. And do not be conformed to this world, but be trans-

formed by the renewing of your mind, that you may
prove what the will of God is, that which is good and
acceptable and perfect.

Romans 12:1, 2

We are to "put off the old man" (Ephesians 4:22 KJV). We are
told to be renewed in the spirit of our mind (v. 23) and to put
on the new man (v. 24). Our minds are to be transformed and
we are to be transformed by the renewing of our minds. This
does affect the soul.

Pray for the Body   How would we pray for the *body?* We
can pray for different parts of the body. In 2 Peter 1:9 we find
that believers can be blinded by Satan. They have forgotten
they had been cleansed. Satan does have power to blind. The
first step to spiritual blindness (blindness of the soul) is neglect
of both the Word and prayer. After a while you will neglect
church—just little by little—for you won't be comfortable
there. In fact, you may be critical of the services. Then you may
gradually drop your Christian friends for others because you
don't have as much in common as you did before. Such a person
is blind and has forgotten he was cleansed.

Christ talks to His doubting disciples and He says, "Having
eyes, do you not see? . . ." (Mark 8:18). This is seeing with the
eyes of the soul. When you really see spiritually, you will see
people's faces as you talk to them. You will be much more aware
of what is going on around you. Your eyes will be tuned in to
God. You will see Him, then others, and also you will really see
yourself and what you are doing.

The next part of the body we can pray for is the *ears*. In the
same verse Jesus says, "Having ears, do you not hear?" In many
places Jesus says, "He that hath ears to hear, let him hear." They
all had *physical* ears. That is not what He meant. He meant the
ears of the soul that first hear God, really hear, and then, as a
result, hear others and self.

The essence of good counseling is to be enabled to hear others and ourselves. As the Holy Spirit tunes us into God, we will see and hear others and ourselves. Many problems can be worked out as we pray for each other and ourselves this way.

We can also pray for the *mind.* "In whose case the god of this world has blinded the minds of the unbelieving, that they might not see the light of the gospel of the glory of Christ, who is the image of God" (2 Corinthians 4:4). Satan can blind minds. "Arm yourselves with the same mind [Christ's]" (*see* 1 Peter 4:1 KJV). ". . . . But we have the mind of Christ" (1 Corinthians 2:16).

Pray for your *mind—conscious* and *subconscious.* The greater part of your mind is subconscious. In fact, your mind has been recording everything that has happened to you since you were conceived.

> For Thou didst form my inward parts;
> Thou didst weave me in my mother's womb.
> I will give thanks to Thee, for I am fearfully
>   and wonderfully made;
> Wonderful are Thy works,
> And my soul knows it very well.
>
> Psalms 139:13, 14

The subconscious controls us. Ask God for honesty, so that as you see and hear yourself and others, you will deal with it honestly.

We can pray for our *hearts.*

> How blessed is the man who fears [reverences] always,
> But he who hardens his heart will fall into calamity.
>
> Proverbs 28:14

We can harden our hearts under God's Word if we want to, but there are bad results. We are told to have a pure heart (Psalms

24:4). This is a cleansed heart! After David's sin with Bathsheba he said, "Create in me a clean heart, O God; and renew a right spirit within me" (Psalms 51:10 KJV). God Himself is the One who does the cleansing (1 John 1:9).

We can pray for our *mouths*. "Let the words of my mouth, and the meditation of my heart, be acceptable in thy sight, O Lord, my strength, and my redeemer" (Psalms 19:14 KJV). We pray that our mouths will be under His control—anointed by Him. Please read James 3, the chapter of the tongue. There are many Scriptures with reference to the tongue. People know what really is in your heart by what you say. To say you are only teasing does not change it. Listen carefully to a person when he is angry. This is the "real" person talking—not a role being played.

We can pray for our *hands*. In Psalms 24:4, we are told to have clean hands as well as a pure heart. We know from James 4:8 that it is as we draw near to God that we realize our hands are dirty and need washing. Hold them up to God, as a child would to an adult—to be washed—and He will wash them. Lift up holy hands (1 Timothy 2:8). He is our holiness. He is our sanctification (1 Corinthians 1:30).

Using Prayer Weapons   Now, let us use the *prayer weapons* for someone's spirit, soul, and body. Let us call this person Mary. This is, of course, not a real name or case. She is going through rebellion toward God and doesn't read and pray anymore.

We first of all commit her to God. Then we want to use the weapons of the Blood shed on the cross. Remember (Exodus 12) that in obedience the blood was applied to a certain area for covering and protection. After we commit her to the Father we apply the Blood to her—spirit, soul, and body. Remember this is not physical blood. This is closet prayer (John 14:12–15). As we pray for her spirit we ask God to refresh and renew her love for Himself: *the Word, prayer, Jesus' coming, love for the brethren,* and *God's House.*

As we apply the Blood to her soul we pray that God will renew her mind and give her soul healing. As David said, "Heal my soul" (*see* Psalms 41:4).

As we *apply the Blood to the body*, we name the different parts of the body and ask for healing in each area. We pray for her *eyes* and *ears* to see and hear God. We cannot make her read her Bible and pray, but when she sees and hears God with the eyes and ears of her soul, she will want to read and pray.

We apply the Blood to her *mind*, conscious and subconscious and ask God to make her honest with Him, with herself, and others. We apply the Blood to her *heart* and ask God to soften it. She has hardened her heart to God and the Word. We ask the Holy Spirit to write across her heart, meeting her particular needs. We apply the Blood to her *mouth* and ask that it be anointed and controlled by Him. We apply the Blood to her *hands* and *feet*, asking that she do the things and go the places God wants her to!

We ask for a *filling of the Spirit*. We are commanded to be filled with the Spirit (Ephesians 5:18). As we yield areas of our lives to Christ, He can then fill them with Himself.

Remember, as you pray, that you are in Christ and you are praying with His faith, His authority, and His power! Satan is defeated. Keep praying and don't give in to despair and discouragement (Luke 18:1).

Ask God to reveal to you how to show love in a tangible way to the one for whom you are praying. Perhaps it will be a favorite cake—or doing something for him that he has wanted. It is God's love pouring through you—He will answer. He has promised!

9

Binding and Loosing

"Truly I say to you, whatever you shall bind on earth shall have been bound in heaven; and whatever you loose on earth shall have been loosed in heaven" (Matthew 18:18). As we studied Matthew 18, we knew we would understand this verse only as it was interpreted in the light of the context. In this chapter, Christ was teaching the forgiveness practiced in body-life.

He cautions us not to cause a child to stumble (Matthew 18:1–6). He is very stern in this and says, "But whoever causes one of these little ones who believe in Me to stumble, it is better for him that a heavy millstone be hung around his neck, and that he be drowned in the depth of the sea" (v. 6).

Jesus gives a general caution on stumbling blocks—people who live carelessly in such a way that those following behind trip over them (v. 7). Furthermore, He tells us that if a certain part of our body is used to pull us Satan's way, it would be better to cut it off than to lose eternal life with Christ (vv. 8, 9).

Jesus then goes back to talking about little children, cautioning again about our relationship with them (v. 10). He tells us here that we are not to "despise" little ones. He also reminds us that God loved the little children so much that their angels behold God's face in heaven.

Verses 11–13 relate His beautiful story of the man who had a hundred sheep. Only ninety-nine returned home one night and he went out and found the one which had gone astray. Here He reminds them that He came to save that which was lost.

He cautions about children again in verse 14: "Thus it is not the will of your Father who is in heaven that one of these little ones perish."

Jesus then gives us a pattern for our actions toward those who do something to hurt us. He teaches us how to handle such a situation and not be controlled by it (vv. 15–18). When someone does something that offends us, we can be so filled with resentment or hostilities (or both) that our reaction toward him controls us. It is possible to be so offended by someone that it affects our work, our eating, and our sleeping. We are known best by our *re*actions, not our actions, and God does not want us controlled by them.

Jesus' Way   Jesus gave the steps for the way out. First, go to your brother and tell him. The Bible itself explains how to do this: "Brethren, even if a man is caught in any trespass, you who are spiritual, restore such a one in a spirit of gentleness; looking to yourselves, lest you too be tempted" (Galatians 6:1). Jesus said, ". . . if he listens to you, you have won your brother" (Matthew 18:15).

The second step, if he does not listen, is listed in the next verse: "But if he does not listen to you, take one or two more with you, so that by the mouth of two or three witnesses every fact may be confirmed." The attitude taught in Galatians 6:1 must be manifest by all who go to visit the offending brother.

The third step, if he does not listen, is found in verse 17: "And if he refuses to listen to them, tell it to the church. . . ." This should be done with the same Christlike attitude–not judging (Matthew 7:1), but just stating facts. None of us can really know why a brother or sister does something offensive and cannot repent. Only God knows.

". . . and if he refuses to listen even to the church, let him be to you as a Gentile and a tax-gatherer. Truly I say to you, whatever you shall bind on earth shall have been bound in heaven; and whatever you loose on earth shall have been loosed in heaven" (Matthew 18:17, 18).

The next two verses are about prayer. "Again I say to you, that if two of you agree on earth about anything that they may ask, it shall be done for them by My Father who is in heaven. For where two or three have gathered together in My name, there I am in their midst" (vv. 19, 20). Verse 18 is interpreted by the verses around it. Verses 15–17 are on offensive behavior and how to deal with it. Verses 19–20 are on prayer—how to pray about these circumstances.

Here the teaching on prayer is that if even two people agree on anything they want to ask, it shall be done. Neither one could be double-minded. They would have to know their own minds and what they wanted to ask for. They would have to be *one mind* in the Spirit.

The context tells us that the thing to be prayed about here is the brother or sister who could not or would not repent of the offensive thing they had done. Jesus Christ tells them how in verse 18. He teaches us that some things are to be bound; some are to be loosed.

Binding in Prayer   Who would you agree to bind in prayer? You would bind the brother or sister who has been dealt with in the steps Christ taught, but has only hardened his heart. This is, of course, closet prayer (*see* Matthew 6:5–7). When you have gone the second mile and turned the other cheek, when you have prayed and prayed over him and there is only hardening of the heart, God says to let go of him and let Him deal with him.

In 1 Samuel 15 we have the story of King Saul becoming impatient as he waited for Samuel to come and offer the sacrifice. He finally disobeyed and offered it himself.

> And Samuel said [to Saul],
>   "Has the Lord as much delight in burnt
>   offerings and sacrifices
>   As in obeying the voice of the Lord?

Behold, to obey is better than sacrifice,
And to heed than the fat of rams."

1 Samuel 15:22

Because of his sins of stubbornness and rebellion (v. 23 KJV), the
kingdom was taken away from him.

Samuel continued to mourn for Saul and what happened to
him. We find that God even regretted that He had made Saul
king (v. 35).

"Now the Lord said to Samuel, 'How long will you grieve over
Saul, since I have rejected him from being king over Israel? Fill
your horn with oil, and go; I will send you to Jesse the Bethlehe-
mite, for I have selected a king for Myself among his sons' "
(1 Samuel 16:1).

Saul had sinned. Because of Samuel's natural love for him, he
continued grieving for him. God had to finally deal with Samuel. Saul had had many opportunities to follow God, but chose
his own way instead. God then let him reap the results of his
own actions.

God had a job for Samuel to do. He wanted a new king
appointed, but Samuel's emotions were still so controlled by his
sorrow over Saul that God could not use him in this condition.
Finally God said, "How long will you grieve over Saul since I
have rejected him?" It brought Samuel up short, and he was
very defensive (1 Samuel 16:2).

We can have like reactions. When we are questioned in an
area in which we feel inadequate, we can become defensive.
Many times we have a need to feel we should have an answer for every situation. When we feel we can't control
what is happening or the conversation that is taking place,
we put up our own defense—we become defensive. A person in that situation will subconsciously put on his own "armor of defense." The voice will change, the face will take on
a different look, and the body will stiffen. In body language
—this person is ready to charge into battle. He may charge

verbally. A person on the defensive has to defend his position, method, role, culture (or whatever it is), and he battles
for it. He has put on his own armor which is fighting his battles *his own way*. We put up walls of defense and retreat
behind them for protection from things that threaten us.
Sometimes our walls are silence—because verbalizing our
thoughts is too threatening and painful.

Samuel answered God, "How can I go? When Saul hears of
it, he will kill me . . ." (1 Samuel 16:2). Samuel had been so
caught up in his own sorrow and loss over Saul that it had
affected his relationship with God. He did not trust God to keep
him safe from harm while he anointed a king. God didn't even
answer him—He just started telling him what He wanted done
and how to go about doing it. It is to Samuel's credit that he
obeyed God and followed His instructions in anointing a new
king (v. 4).

Paul writes:

> Keeping faith and a good conscience, which some have
> rejected and suffered shipwreck in regard to their faith.
> Among these are Hymenaeus and Alexander, whom I
> have delivered over to Satan, so that they may be taught
> not to blaspheme.
>
>   1 Timothy 1:19, 20

> But avoid worldly and empty chatter, for it will lead to
> further ungodliness, and their talk will spread like gan-
> grene. Among them are Hymenaeus and Philetus, men
> who have gone astray from the truth saying that the
> resurrection has already taken place, and thus they upset
> the faith of some.
>
>   2 Timothy 2:16–18

I'm sure Paul had dealt with them in kindness. He wrote in
Ephesians: "Be ye kind . . ." (4:32 KJV). I'm sure he had turned

the other cheek and gone the second mile. I'm sure he was not controlled by the emotion of judging. He did what God told Samuel to do. He let go of them and let them reap the results of their own unbelief.

Paul also says, "Alexander the coppersmith did me much harm; the Lord will repay him according to his deeds. Be on guard against him yourself, for he vigorously opposed our teaching" (2 Timothy 4:14, 15). He simply turned him over to God —He is the Judge.

Paul writes about the sin of immorality among the Corinthians. One of the men has been living with his father's wife. Paul says, "I have decided to deliver such a one to Satan for the destruction of his flesh, that his spirit may be saved in the day of the Lord Jesus" (1 Corinthians 5:5). His body was turned over to Satan because of his sin—his spirit was Christ's. We read further on: "But let a man examine himself, and so let him eat of the bread and drink of the cup. For he who eats and drinks, eats and drinks judgment to himself, if he does not judge the body rightly. For this reason many among you are weak and sick, and a number sleep" (1 Corinthians 11:28–30). Paul says that sin unjudged in a believer's life can end in sickness or death. Sin sown in a body produces a harvest of sin.

Jesus says we can bind this person—this offensive one who is determined to go his own way (Matthew 18:18). We will not have to pray this prayer often. We apply the Blood shed on the cross to that person—spirit, soul, and body (1 Thessalonians 5:23), and command in the heavenlies that this person not be able to affect the testimony of the church and the members. We then pray for a work of the Holy Spirit in the church—in cleansing, healing power.

"No weapon that is formed against you shall prosper;
And every tongue that accuses you in judgment you will
    condemn.

This is the heritage of the servants of the Lord,
And their vindication is from Me," declares the Lord.

Isaiah 54:17

Condemn the Tongue   God says, "Whatever you shall bind
. . . whatever you shall loose." He doesn't tell us to ask Him to
do it. He says in the above verse from Isaiah that *you* condemn
their tongues. He doesn't say to ask Him to condemn their
tongues.

This one we are to pray for is a person who has wrongly
judged us. We have prayed, gone the second mile, turned the
other cheek, and forgiven that person. Still there has been no
change. We are to condemn his tongue. This does not hurt the
person physically. We apply the Blood to his tongue and condemn it as we stand complete in Christ. We thank God that no
weapon formed against us shall prosper. A network of lies is a
weapon. Remember, Satan uses fiery darts. There are other
darts also—darts of envy, jealousy, and so on. David asked God
to deliver him from the strife of tongues:

Thou dost hide them in the secret place of Thy presence
    from the conspiracies of man;
Thou dost keep them secretly in a shelter from the strife
    of tongues.

Psalms 31:20

"You will be hidden from the scourge of the tongue, Neither
will you be afraid of violence when it comes" (Job 5:21). Sometimes we need to be delivered from people's tongues.

Loosing in Prayer   Who would we loose? We would loose
those who are bound by Satan. Jesus was accused of casting out
demons with Satan's power (Matthew 12). "And if Satan casts
out Satan, he is divided against himself; how then shall his king-

dom stand? And if I by Beelzebul cast out demons, by whom do your sons cast them out? Consequently they shall be your judges. But if I cast out demons by the Spirit of God, then the kingdom of God has come upon you" (vv. 26–28). He was explaining that if Satan casts out Satan, his kingdom will fall. He adds, "Or how can anyone enter the strong man's house and carry off his property, unless he first binds the strong man? And then he will plunder his house" (v. 29).

As we apply the Blood to the unbeliever's spirit, soul, and body, we loose him from Satan's power. He is completely bound by Satan. We must bind Satan and must loose the unbeliever. We rebuke Satan (James 4:7) in Jesus' Name and command him to leave that person alone. Pray for his spirit, his soul (for healing), and all the parts of his body. As you pray for his eyes and ears, ask God to open them to see and hear Him. When people really see and hear God, they will then see their need of a Saviour. We do not really see our need until we see Him.

Pray for his mind—loosing it from Satan's power. Loose the heart from Satan's power and pray that he might not be able to harden his heart. Bind or apply the Blood to the unbeliever completely, committing him to God. Trust the Holy Spirit to do the finished work in him. Remember the chapter on fruit. As we are one spirit with Christ, there will be fruit—lasting fruit from this union.

We need to use our authority and power in Christ and do the works that He did. We need to bind Satan's influence in the lives of others and loose them from his power.

Illness   Christ healed the woman who had been bent double for eighteen years. He was condemned by an official for doing it on the Sabbath (Luke 13:10–14). He replied, "And ought not this woman, being a daughter of Abraham, whom Satan hath bound, lo, these eighteen years, be loosed from this bond on the sabbath day?" (v. 16 KJV).

I do not mean to imply that all illnesses are from Satan. Illness is a result of the Fall (Genesis 3). However, we believe we should be open to the truth from this verse—this particular illness was from Satan.

We believe today that we, as Christians, are naive about Satan's tactics. Romans 8:28 is a cornerstone verse for our lives. However, we do not accept circumstances or illnesses as being from God until we have prayed over them. We apply the Blood to the person who is ill. We rebuke spirits of illness and disease (*see* Matthew 4:23, 24) and command them to leave if any of the illness is from Satan.

Illness and disease can be fiery darts from Satan, trying to get past our shield of faith. They can also be from demons of illness and disease which can be within. If you pray and there is no response, you may need special counseling for that person.

Please do not accuse another of having demons. People's illnesses do control other lives and there can be deep pools of bitterness and resentment over the cost of the illness and the inconveniences caused. It is unkind and unscriptural to judge another person's illness.

We also thank God for His will in our lives. This opens our bodies and minds for healing. Satan can have no victory as we stand in Christ. Remember, He is our armor. Thanksgiving to God removes any guilt over an illness, and this is very important. Guilt over the medical bills, days lost at work, or inconvenience to the family can intensify the illness and compound the problems.

And having summoned His twelve disciples, He gave them authority over unclean spirits, to cast them out, and to heal every kind of disease and every kind of sickness.

Matthew 10:1

And He called the twelve together, and gave them power and authority over all the demons, and to heal diseases.

Luke 9:1

Christ said, Behold, I give unto you power. . . .

Luke 10:19 KJV

But ye shall receive power. . . .

Acts 1:8 KJV

In these passages and others, Christ gives us the command to go and be His witnesses. He gives us the power and authority to do it. He puts His own armor on us for the battle. His armor is Himself, and He goes before us. Christ does the fighting, for the battle is His, not ours. He promises to do the works through us as we pray, believing with His faith.

Hidden in Christ   Scripture tells how Daniel's three friends, Shadrach, Meshach, and Abednego, had been bound and put into the fiery furnace because of their faith in God (Daniel 3). As King Nebuchadnezzar looked into the flames, he saw four men walking around and the fourth was "like the Son of God" (v. 25 KJV). The men who had been bound were walking around. They were lifted out, and all were startled by the miracle. Their hair was not singed and their clothing was not burned. There was not even the smell of smoke about them. Absolutely nothing was changed except that they had been bound and they were now loosed. The only thing the fiery furnace had done was to burn off the things that bound them.

This is true of our fiery-furnace experiences. As Christ walks with us, as we are hidden in Him, nothing can touch us. The only thing touched and removed will be the chains that bind us to the old life.

Jesus' beloved friend Lazarus had died (John 11). He had gone to the tomb with Lazarus's sisters, Mary and Martha, and their friends. Jesus knew that He was going to raise him from the dead. He prayed to God the Father and then called Lazarus forth from his grave. The Scriptures relate that he came forth bound hand and foot with wrappings. Even his face was bound with wrappings. Jesus said, "Loose him, and let him go" (v. 44 KJV). I can imagine the reactions. Martha had already told Christ that Lazarus had been dead for four days and that by now he would have the terrible odor of a decaying body. The odor had probably saturated the graveclothes—and now, Christ was saying, "Loose him."

Probably some would have said, "Being around death makes me sick." Or perhaps, "I can't stand the smell," or even, "I'm too busy. I've an appointment to keep." Another might have replied, "Lord, removing graveclothes isn't my gift."

Being around those bound by Satan isn't pleasant. They have the smell of death on them. Christ tells us to loose them. Lazarus could not walk until he was loosed. In fact, he probably would have died if he had not been loosed. His physical life depended on those around him. Other people's spiritual life depends upon us.

Many around us are bound in sin. Some are completely bound by Satan. Some believers are bound in certain areas of their lives, such as adultery, lies, bitterness, and so on. These also need to be loosed, and as they are loosed they need the Holy Spirit's filling.

> Is not this the fast that I have chosen? to loose the bands of wickedness, to undo the heavy burdens, and to let the oppressed go free, and that ye break every yoke.
>
> Isaiah 58:6 KJV

> . . . he hath sent me to bind up the brokenhearted, to proclaim liberty to the captives, and the opening of the prison to them that are bound.
>
> Isaiah 61:1 KJV

This is speaking of Christ—loosing those who are bound. We are to do the works He did (John 14:10–15). As we enter into His work, souls are freed. Remember, this is not done with our human love. We do not have enough love in ourselves. It is His love through us (Romans 5:5).

Just a word of caution: As the disciples returned to Jesus after laboring for the Lord, they were excited that the demons were subject to them (Luke 10:17). Jesus said, "Notwithstanding in this rejoice not, that the spirits are subject unto you; but rather rejoice, because your names are written in heaven" (v. 20 KJV).

You will see lives changed; you will see people saved as you work together with Him. He will be glorified!